VITAL SIGNS
2011

ISBN: 978-1-878071-98-9

Worldwatch Institute
1776 Massachusetts Avenue, NW
Suite 800
Washington, DC 20036
U.S.A.

This book is printed on paper 50% recycled, including 25% post-consumer waste, FSC certified, and elemental chlorine-free.

VITAL SIGNS

2011

The Trends That Are Shaping Our Future

WORLDWATCH INSTITUTE

Gary Gardner, *Project Director*

Erik Assadourian
Vanessa Damelio
Robert Engelman
Alice McKeown Jaspersen
Nausheen Khan
Saya Kitasei
Petra Löw
Shakuntala Makhijani
John Mulrow

Alexander Ochs
Stephanie Pappas
Michael Renner
James Russell
Kelsey Russell
Samuel Shrank
Matt Styslinger
Alexandra Tung

Linda Starke, *Editor*
Lyle Rosbotham, *Designer*

Worldwatch Institute, Washington, DC

Contents

TECHNICAL NOTE

Units of measure throughout this book are metric unless common usage dictates otherwise, Historical data series in *Vital Signs* are updated in each edition, incorporating any revisions by originating organizations. Unless noted otherwise, references to regions or groupings of countries follow definitions of the Statistics Division of the U.N. Department of Economic and Social Affairs. Data expressed in U.S. dollars have for the most part been deflated (see endnotes for specific details for each trend).

Acknowledgments

Vital Signs is a team effort, involving writers and researchers, of course, but also many individuals and organizations in diverse roles. Providing the needed support for this team are our funders—the foundations, governments, international agencies, and individuals who understand the value of tracking trends that inform policymakers and the public about the prospects for sustainable economies.

Over the last year this group has included the American Clean Skies Foundation; the Apollo Alliance Project with funding provided by the Rockefeller and Surdna Foundations; the Heinrich Böll Foundation; the Casten Family Foundation; the Compton Foundation, Inc.; the Del Mar Global Trust; the Energy and Environment Partnership with Central America (EEP); the Bill and Melinda Gates Foundation; the Ministry of Foreign Affairs of the Government of Finland; Sam Gary and Associates, Inc.; the German Federal Ministry for the Environment, Nature Protection and Nuclear Safety; the German Society for International Cooperation (GIZ); the Hitz Foundation; the Steven C. Leuthold Family Foundation; the MAP Royalty, Inc. Sustainable Energy Education Fellowship Program; the Renewable Energy & Energy Efficiency Partnership (REEEP); the Shenandoah Foundation; the Laney Thornton Foundation; the United Nations Foundation; the United Nations Population Fund (UNFPA); the Wallace Genetic Foundation, Inc.; the Wallace Global Fund; the Johanette Wallerstein Institute; the Weeden Foundation; and the Winslow Foundation.

The Shared Earth Foundation and Doug and Barbara Engmann provided dedicated support for *Vital Signs Online*, the Web version of this book. And a generous grant from the Richard and Rhoda Goldman Fund supports the communications and outreach efforts for *Vital Signs Online*. We are also grateful for the support of the Friends of Worldwatch, whose generosity underwrites nearly a third of our operating budget. And we extend a special note of thanks to the Worldwatch Board of Directors, the ever-supportive stewards of the Worldwatch mission.

Worldwatch relies on its cadre of dedicated researchers who follow trends year round. Special thanks is given to in-house researchers who contributed pieces to this volume, including Erik Assadourian, Robert Engelman, Saya Kitasei, Alice McKeown Jaspersen, John Mulrow, Alexander Ochs, Samuel Shrank, and Michael Renner. We also appreciate the contributions of outside experts James Russell and Petra Löw, as well as the pieces authored by our hardworking interns Vanessa Damello, Nausheen Khan, Shakuntala Makhijani, Stephanie Pappas, Kelsey Russell, Matt Styslinger, and Alexandra Tung.

Vital Signs authors receive help from reviewers and other experts who offer insights on the trends we follow. We give particular thanks this year to Zoë Chafe, Colin Couchman, Wally Falcon, Carl Haub, Samir KC, Vello Kuuskraa, Wolfgang Lutz, Elizabeth Madsen, Tobias Plieninger, Janet Sawin, Steven Tobin, and Raymond Torres.

The online parent of *Vital Signs, Vital Signs*

Online, turned one year old in 2010. I am especially indebted to my predecessor, Alice McKeown Jaspersen, for her leadership in establishing the online offering and for handing off to me a well-organized project. Her administrative, management, and research skills are legendary.

A cadre of staff works behind the scenes to ensure that our work is funded, distributed, and read. For their extensive but often unheralded efforts I am grateful to Alex Kostura, Colleen Kredell, Trudy Loo, Mary Redfern, Patricia Shyne, and Russell Simon of our communications, marketing, and development departments and to their predecessors for their contributions in 2010: Ben Block, Juliane Diamond, Darcey Rakestraw, and Julia Tier.

As always, we acknowledge and thank Linda Starke, whose edits clarify and polish our prose, and Lyle Rosbotham, our graphic designer, whose artistry gives beauty and accessibility to our collection of trends.

Enjoy *Vital Signs 2011,* and stay up to date on the latest sustainability trends throughout the year at vitalsigns.worldwatch.org.

Gary Gardner
Project Director
Worldwatch Institute
1776 Massachusetts Avenue, N.W.
Washington, DC 20036
vitalsigns.worldwatch.org

Preface

The Great Recession has cast a long but punctuated shadow across many of the trends the Worldwatch Institute tracks. Most global economic indicators show the unmistakable effects of the sharpest economic contraction since the Great Depression. But some major economies have emerged relatively unscathed. Sectors like automobile manufacturing shrank precipitously, but renewable energy continued to follow the robust growth path that began in the mid-2000s. Some environmental trends have worsened, but many countries have adopted encouraging new environmental policies and laws. The gradual and uneven advance toward sustainable economies is already showing new signs of life as the Great Recession winds down.

The mixed nature of economic, environmental, and social trends shaping our world is clear from this edition of *Vital Signs*. Gross world economic output increased by just 0.3 percent in 2009, a substantial slowdown from the 2000–08 average yearly increase of 6.6 percent. Trade volumes fell by nearly 11 percent. But performance varied widely, with some of the richest countries experiencing the sharpest dips. Whereas advanced economies contracted by 2 percent in 2009, emerging and developing economies grew at a relatively robust 3.3 percent. And the largest emerging economies continued to expand rapidly: China's by 9.1 percent, for example, and India's by 7.4 percent.

Global roundwood production fell by more than 4 percent in 2009—the largest percentage drop in nearly half a century—as the recession hit wood-intensive industries, especially housing. Meanwhile, global production of cars and light trucks dropped 13 percent in 2009, the second consecutive year of declines. One silver lining: in Japan, the Toyota Prius was the best-selling car in 2009, marking the first time a hybrid vehicle has topped annual auto sales.

Unfortunately, climate change did not pause for the recession. Last year—the warmest on record—produced more glacial and polar ice melt and expanded the water volume, which raised the level of the world's oceans. From 1993 to 2009, sea level rose 3.0 millimeters (mm) per year—a much faster annual rate than the 1.7 mm figure during the preceding 118 years.

More frequent and violent storms were another notable feature of 2009. While it remains difficult to connect most specific weather events definitively to climate change, increased storm intensity and more frequent floods and droughts are among the impacts that most climate models indicate will result from the dramatic changes in Earth's atmosphere now under way.

In the energy realm, renewable sources have fared better than conventional ones in the recession. Solar photovoltaic capacity increased by 20 percent in 2009, and solar thermal power plant capacity rose by 26 percent. Solar energy now provides about 1 percent of the electricity in Germany and more than 2 percent in Spain. Meanwhile, the slight slowing in demand growth compared with 2008 contributed to a historic decline in solar module prices of nearly 40 percent. The improved economics caused market growth to accelerate dramatically in 2010.

Meanwhile, global wind power capacity grew more than 31 percent in 2009, the highest rate in eight years—with China emerging as the world's largest market for wind turbines. Wind power accounted for about 2 percent of global electricity use in 2009. And biofuel production increased by 9.6 percent, although this was a far smaller growth than the nearly 44 percent jump from 2007 to 2008, largely due to the world-wide recession and lower Brazilian production. Biofuels accounted for 2 percent of all transport fuels, up from 1.8 percent in 2008.

At the same time, global use of coal contracted by just under 0.5 percent in 2009, while natural gas consumption dropped by 2.1 percent, the largest recorded one-year decline. This reflects the recession-driven decline in demand in North America and Europe, the largest gas consumers. Coal use fell sharply there, and it is now likely that both regions have passed their peak in coal combustion. Coal use grew robustly in China (up. 9.6 percent) and India (up 8.4 percent) in 2009, however, contributing to a rise in international coal prices.

For the second year in a row, global nuclear generating capacity dropped slightly in 2009, largely because aging nuclear power plants are no longer producing as much power as they once did. The addition of new plants in India and Japan was offset by plant retirements in Japan and Lithuania.[3]

The steady erosion of the planet's biodiversity continued in 2009, with the addition of 365 species to the "threatened" category of the Red List maintained by the International Union for Conservation of Nature, a 2.1 percent increase. Only 2 species were removed from the threatened category. Some 36 percent of animal, plant, and fungi species are now considered threatened.

Yet government conservation initiatives in recent years have been encouraging. At the 10th Conference of the Parties to the Convention on Biological Diversity in Nagoya, Japan, in October 2010, governments adopted a 10-year Strategic Plan to guide national and international conservation efforts as well as a new treaty to govern the sharing of benefits associated with genetic resources. They also agreed on a plan to increase levels of official development assistance in support of biodiversity.

In the food and agriculture sector, the recession's greatest impact was seen in fertilizer consumption, which fell by 7.5 percent in 2008, the sharpest annual decline in nearly 50 years of data collection. The decline was a direct response to price spikes in 2007 and 2008 that caused demand to fall. The drop in fertilizer consumption did not translate into a decline in food production, however. Farmers produced a near-record crop of grains at more than 2.25 billion tons, a 21-percent increase since 2000, as they continue to coax greater yields from a relatively stable supply of agricultural land. Meat production also increased, but by a relatively sluggish 0.8 percent in 2009 compared with the 2.4 percent growth rate of 2008. Since 2000, global meat production has risen by 20 percent.

Environmental issues lapped at the edge of the agricultural sector, however. In 2010, a heat wave in Russia destroyed nearly 10 million hectares of crops—causing Russia, one of the world's largest wheat exporters, to suspend all exports, which immediately drove up global grain prices.

The world's faltering progress in the effort to build sustainable societies is clearly not good enough. Scientists believe that the window of opportunity for dealing with our sustainability challenges is closing quickly. A 2009 "planetary boundaries" study on nine natural systems found that safe operating boundaries for human activity have likely already been crossed for climate change, nitrogen cycling, and biodiversity protection. Recession or not, governments and people throughout the world will need to do a lot more if we are to leave a stable economy and a healthy planet for future generations.

Christopher Flavin
President

Gary Gardner
Project Director

Energy and Transportation Trends

Satellite image by GeoEye

The Beijing South Railway Station, opened in 2008, can handle 30,000 passengers per hour.

For additional energy and transportation trends, go to vitalsigns.worldwatch.org.

Global Coal Use Stagnates Despite Growing Chinese and Indian Markets

Saya Kitasei

Global use of coal fell by just under 0.5 percent in 2009 to 3,278 million tons of oil equivalent (mtoe) from the all-time high of 3,286 mtoe in 2008, interrupting the trend of rapid growth—an average of 4.3 percent annually—that has defined global coal markets over the last decade.[1] (See Figure 1.) The global commodity boom that drove coal consumption and prices up in 2008 ended, sending prices plummeting over 40 percent in some markets.[2] (See Figure 2.)

The decline in consumption reflected diverging trends in North America, Europe, and Japan on the one hand, where the recession, low natural gas prices, and environmental concerns drove coal use down at least 10 percent, and China and India on the other hand, where coal demand remained strong.[3] Because these two major coal-dependent economies buffered global coal markets against the recession, use of coal fell less than use of any other fossil fuel, and coal's share of global primary energy consumption rose to 29.4 percent in 2009, its highest level since 1970.[4]

China continued to be the largest and one of the fastest-growing coal markets in the world, with usage rising 9.6 percent to 1,537 mtoe in 2009, or 46.9 percent of total world coal consumption.[5] The increase in coal use in China between 2008 and 2009 was greater than the total 2009 usage in Germany and Poland combined.[6] In 2009, China became a net importer of coal for the first time, thanks to a surge in imports of steam coal (the grade used in boilers for electricity generation) from Australia, Indonesia, and Viet Nam.[7] In part, this was due to growing profit opportunities for buying imported coal, the price of which was depressed in response to reduced global demand, and then reselling it domestically, where prices remained relatively high thanks to strong demand and government policies designed to limit domestic production and shore up prices.[8]

India, like China, saw strong growth in coal consumption and production in 2009, up 6.8 and 8.4 percent, respectively, to 246 mtoe and 212 mtoe.[9] Rising electricity demand is already outpacing growth in domestic supplies, and

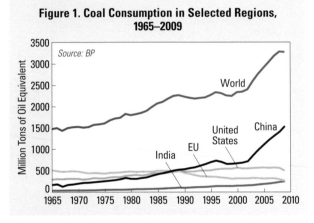

Figure 1. Coal Consumption in Selected Regions, 1965–2009

Source: BP

Figure 2. Coal Prices, 1990–2009

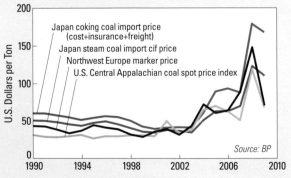

Japan coking coal import price (cost+insurance+freight)
Japan steam coal import cif price
Northwest Europe marker price
U.S. Central Appalachian coal spot price index

Source: BP

some analysts believe that India's existing and planned coal plants could require almost all of the country's recoverable resources over their lifetimes.[10] India passed Taiwan last year to become the fourth largest importer of coal.[11]

Japan, which has very few indigenous resources of coal, maintained its position as the world's leading importer in 2009.[12] As with many other countries in the Organisation for Economic Co-operation and Development, however, Japan's electricity demand fell sharply, and coal consumption fell even more sharply, plummeting 15.2 percent from 2008 levels.[13] (See Figure 3.)

In the United States, home of the largest proven coal reserves in the world, coal consumption was down 11.5 percent in 2009 to 498 mtoe.[14] Production also fell 9.3 percent, to 540 mtoe.[15] In large part, this decline was due to reduced demand from the power sector, which uses 93.6 percent of all coal consumed in the country.[16] Demand from coke plants, which produce iron and steel, dropped 30.6 percent thanks to slowed manufacturing.[17] While overall electricity generation declined, coal's share fell as well, from 48.2 to 44.6 percent, displaced mainly by natural gas and renewable energy.[18] In anticipation of tightening regulations on power plant emissions and the higher generating costs that would result, some utilities have begun planning to retire their older, less efficient coal plants.[19]

Coal's falling market share in the United States can also be attributed to the stiff opposition that new plants have faced from groups concerned about the environmental and health impacts of mines and power plants.[20] In April 2010, the U.S. Environmental Protection Agency announced stronger environmental permitting requirements for surface coal mining in Appalachia, where a controversial technique called mountaintop removal has been responsible for burying adjacent streams.[21]

In the European Union, coal consumption fell 10.8 percent to 261 mtoe, with Germany, the United Kingdom, and Poland experiencing the largest drops.[22] Germany and Poland also

reported declining hard coal production for the sixth consecutive year.[23] As in the United States, reduced demand for electricity, steel, and iron brought on by the recession is responsible for a major part of this reduction. Policies are also playing a role in reducing European demand for coal, however. In May 2010, the European Commission proposed making this the last year in which subsidies for coal mines and power plants would be permitted in the European Union, with very limited extensions until 2014.[24]

Russia, home to the world's second largest proven reserves of coal, used 83 mtoe in 2009, which was 17.2 percent less than in 2008.[25] Its production also fell 8.1 percent, but exports rose

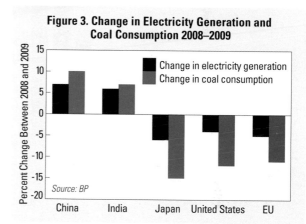

Figure 3. Change in Electricity Generation and Coal Consumption 2008–2009

Source: BP

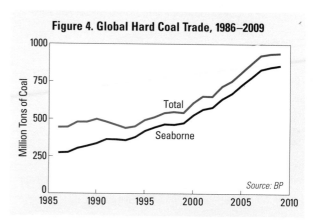

Figure 4. Global Hard Coal Trade, 1986–2009

Source: BP

to serve the Chinese market.[26] Over the past decade, Russia has attempted to increase the use of coal in its electricity sector in order to free up natural gas for lucrative export.[27] Nevertheless, the share of coal in Russia's primary energy use fell from 14.7 to 13.0 percent between 2008 and 2009, far below the world average.[28]

In Australia, consumption of coal fell 0.9 percent to 51 mtoe, while production rose 3.7 percent to 228 mtoe.[29] But Australia led the world in coal exports in 2009, despite producing only

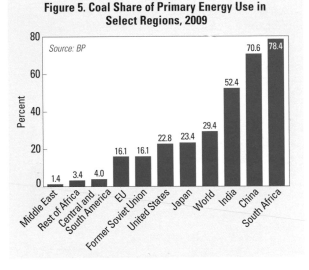

Figure 5. Coal Share of Primary Energy Use in Select Regions, 2009

Source: BP

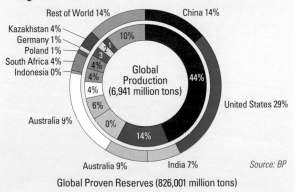

Figure 6. Coal Production and Proven Reserves, 2009

Rest of World 14%   China 14%
Kazakhstan 4%
Germany 1%
Poland 1%
South Africa 4%
Indonesia 0%

Global Production (6,941 million tons)

10%
3
4%
4%
4%
6%
0%
14%
44%

Australia 9%
United States 29%

Australia 9%   India 7%   *Source: BP*

Global Proven Reserves (826,001 million tons)

6.7 percent of global output.[30] The country exported some 66 percent of the coal it produced in 2009, more than 40 percent of which went to Japan, its largest customer.[31] The volume of global seaborne trade in coal has almost doubled over the last 10 years, and it accounts for 91 percent of total trade in coal, compared to 68 percent in 1990.[32] (See Figure 4.) This expanding seaborne trade has begun to connect previously isolated coal markets.[33]

South Africa's coal production passed Russia's in 2009, reaching 141 mtoe.[34] Consumption fell 3 percent from 2008 levels, to 99 mtoe.[35] Whereas coal accounts for 78 percent of South Africa's primary energy use, it does not currently play a large role elsewhere in Africa, accounting for only 3.4 percent of the rest of the continent's primary energy use.[36] Central and South America similarly rely on coal for only 4 percent of their energy needs, and the Middle East obtains only 1.4 percent of its energy from coal.[37] (See Figure 5.)

Coal's perceived abundance, which has been a major argument for continuing to depend on it, is now being questioned. Although South Africa holds 3.7 percent of the world's proven coal reserves (a 122-year supply at current rates of production), some analysts believe that this country could reach peak coal as early as 2020.[38] This is because demand is expected to increase, with the government bringing 3,800 megawatts of coal generation back into service and constructing a new 4,800-megawatt coal power plant to alleviate the country's electricity shortages.[39] China—which produced almost one out of every two tons of world coal in 2009 and which has the third highest proven coal reserves (after the United States and Russia)—has only enough proven coal reserves for 38 years of production at 2009 rates.[40] (See Figure 6.) Expectations of scarcity in the decades ahead have encouraged the Chinese government to invest heavily in alternative sources of energy.

In recent years, coal's primacy in many power sectors around the world has also been criticized because of its high contribution to greenhouse gas emissions. From 2002 to 2007, carbon dioxide (CO_2) emissions from coal grew by an average of 6.1 percent annually, and in 2004 coal surpassed oil to become the largest contributor to global CO_2 emissions of the fossil fuels.[41] Although environmental and health concerns have driven investment in technologies that can lower coal's carbon footprint, including cofiring biomass in power plants and capturing and storing the carbon dioxide that plants produce, coal will face an uphill battle to maintain its market share in the years ahead.

Growth of Biofuel Production Slows

Samuel Shrank

Global biofuel production rose in 2009 to a total of 92.8 billion liters from 84.7 billion liters in 2008, a 9.6-percent increase.[1] (See Figure 1.) This was a far smaller increase than the nearly 44 percent jump from 2007 to 2008, largely due to the worldwide recession and lower Brazilian production.[2] With worldwide oil production falling 2.6 percent from 2008 to 2009, biofuels accounted for 2 percent of all transport fuel, up from 1.8 percent in 2008.[3]

Biofuels are alternatives to gasoline, diesel, and other transport fuels that are derived from biomass. The two most common biofuels are ethanol, made by fermenting the sugars in plant material, and biodiesel, made from oils and fats. In 2009 the world produced 76.2 billion liters of ethanol and 16.6 billion liters of biodiesel.[4]

The United States and Brazil produce the largest amount of ethanol, roughly 41 billion and 26.3 billion liters respectively, which account for 88 percent of the world total.[5] Other producers include China, Canada, France, and Germany, but none supplies more than 3 per-

cent of the total.[6] U.S. ethanol production continued to grow in 2009, up 16 percent from 2008, and represented 54 percent of the world total.[7] The U.S. industry, still dominated by corn-based ethanol, looks poised for further growth as well. As of January 2010, biorefinery additions and expansions that would produce an additional 5.5 billion liters a year were under construction.[8]

Brazilian ethanol production fell 3 percent from 2008 to 2009 but still accounted for 35 percent of worldwide production.[9] Brazilian ethanol is almost completely derived from sugarcane; unusually high sugar prices and poor weather in key growing regions combined to force down supply.[10] Domestic demand for ethanol continues to increase, however, so Brazilian production will likely return to its previous growth path.[11] Ethanol production in the rest of the world increased by 26 percent, with strong growth in Canada, France, and Germany and a doubling in smaller producers such as the United Kingdom and Belgium.[12]

Some 16.6 billion liters of biodiesel were produced in 2009, up 9 percent from 2008. [13] This growth is far lower than the annual average over the previous five years of 51 percent, however.[14] European Union (EU) countries retained their dominant position, with almost 50 percent of the global total, led by France and Germany with 2.6 billion liters each.[15] (See Figure 2.) The largest biodiesel producers outside the EU were the United States, Brazil, and Argentina.[16]

One of the main drivers behind biofuel growth is the national use mandates and support policies in the United States, the European Union, and many countries around the world. The U.S. Renewable Fuels Standard was revised in 2010 in response to the 2007 Energy Independence and Security Act (EISA). The Envi-

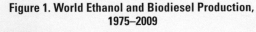

Figure 1. World Ethanol and Biodiesel Production, 1975–2009

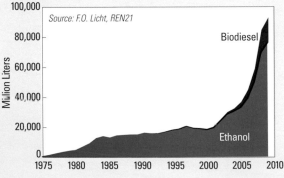

Source: F.O. Licht, REN21

ronmental Protection Agency (EPA) announced that corn-based ethanol produced in a natural-gas-fired facility met the new requirement that biofuels must have 20 percent lower lifecycle greenhouse gas emissions than gasoline, even when accounting for indirect land use change.[17] This perhaps ends the debate, at least inside the U.S. government, over whether ethanol has higher greenhouse gas emissions than gasoline.

Meeting this requirement ensures that U.S. demand for corn-based ethanol will be able to continue growing, as it will be eligible to count toward the renewable fuel mandate, which grows from 42 billion liters in 2009 to 136 billion in 2022.[18] EPA also recently announced that it will allow the maximum blend of ethanol in standard gasoline to rise from 10 to 15 percent for cars from model year 2007 and newer.[19] Most gas stations cannot carry more than one fuel blend, however, and with a ruling on model years 2001–2006 yet to come, and with no prospect for the inclusion of cars from model years 2000 and earlier, the impact of this ruling may be slight.[20] Moreover, the market for corn-based ethanol will be hurt if the tax credit of 45¢ a gallon for blending ethanol with gasoline and the import tariff of 54¢ a gallon for other forms of ethanol are allowed to expire at the end of 2010.

EISA also requires that 80 billion liters come from advanced biofuels by 2022, with no more than half the greenhouse gas emissions of gasoline.[21] Similarly, the EU's mandate for all member states to get 10 percent of transport fuel from biofuels by 2020 is contingent on the development of "sustainable, second-generation biofuels" by that time.[22]

Second-generation biofuels, as they are commonly known, can be made from a wide variety of biomass sources. The two types getting the most attention are cellulosic ethanol, which involves extracting sugars for fermentation from the cellulosic material found in all plants, and synthetic fuel, for which biomass is gasified to create synthesis gas, which can be converted to ethanol, diesel, or other fuels.[23] The flexibility of these processes allows for the use of feed-

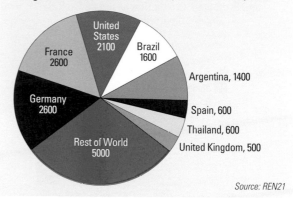

Figure 2. Biodiesel Production, Million Liters, 2009

United States 2100
Brazil 1600
France 2600
Argentina, 1400
Germany 2600
Spain, 600
Thailand, 600
Rest of World 5000
United Kingdom, 500

Source: REN21

stocks that would otherwise be considered waste—woodchips, pulp, husks, and stems—or that would have little value as cultivated crops—switchgrass, jatropha, and short-rotation poplar, for example.[24]

There are both economic and environmental reasons why the United States, the European Union, and other countries are trying to promote the growth of second-generation biofuels. The variety of possible feedstocks means that these biofuels do not rely on food crops and can be harvested from degraded and marginal land that could not be used for food production.[25] Yields are higher on fertile land for all second-generation biofuel feedstocks, however, so reliance on the newer biofuels would not completely eliminate competition for land with food crops.[26] And even use on marginal land could lead to competition with forage production for livestock.[27]

Many second-generation biofuels are also associated with far lower greenhouse gas emissions than corn- or sugarcane-based ethanol because of their higher feedstock yields, efficient conversion from feedstock to ethanol and biodiesel, and feedstocks with higher potential as greenhouse gas sinks.[28] Some feedstocks, specifically low-input high-diversity grass mixtures and woody crops such as poplar, act as carbon sinks even without counting the displaced fossil fuel use due to their ability to sequester carbon.[29] Despite higher yields, projections of

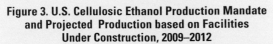

Figure 3. U.S. Cellulosic Ethanol Production Mandate and Projected Production based on Facilities Under Construction, 2009–2012

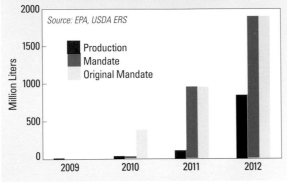

the use of second-generation biofuels under aggressive climate policy regimes involve the dedication of up to 15 percent of all arable land by 2050 and 25 percent by 2100.[30] Expansion of second-generation biofuels could therefore have negative implications for food security, biodiversity conservation, and water supply.[31]

The growth of second-generation biofuels is currently being held back by high production and capital costs.[32] The United States cut its 2010 mandate for cellulosic biofuel from 379 million liters to 25 million, and production is projected to be roughly 38 million liters.[33] There are roughly 50 pilot, demonstration, and commercial plants in the United States that will be producing second-generation biofuels by 2012, but projected capacity will still fall far short of EISA mandates for both cellulosic ethanol and advanced biofuels more generally.[34] (See Figure 3.) Capital investment costs for second-generation biofuel plants are thought to be three to four times those of first-generation biofuel plants, and production costs are higher as well.[35] At least in the United States, higher production costs are somewhat mitigated by subsidies in the 2008 Farm Bill, however.[36]

Both research and production of second-generation biofuels is concentrated in North America and Europe, although this may change as the industry expands and the need for land grows.[37] Long-term projections show most production in the United States, Latin America, and Africa, where agricultural land is more readily available.[38] The pilot, demonstration, and commercial plants currently operating mostly use industrial byproducts and agricultural wastes as their feedstock, though many technologies based on dedicated energy crops are in development.[39] Three commercial-scale second-generation biofuel plants are slated to open in 2010 in the United States and the Netherlands, and roughly a dozen more are scheduled to begin operation by 2012.[40] One estimate of 2014 capacity is 8.8 billion liters.[41] Though this represents tremendous growth, it suggests that second-generation biofuels will remain a small portion of overall biofuel production for the next few years.

Third-generation biofuels, derived from algae, have recently drawn attention as well. The advantages of microalgae and macroalgae (seaweed) include a fast growth rate, high carbon uptake, and lack of competition with other crops.[42] Countries including South Korea, the United Kingdom, Chile, Japan, and the Philippines have announced plans to invest heavily in research and development on third-generation biofuels.[43] Commercial-scale production is years away, however, as costs need to come down and experience is needed in commercializing what has only ever been a wild crop.[44]

Despite concerns over the environmental impact and effect on food security in developing countries, biofuel production is expected to continue growing.[45] Estimates go as high as 100 percent growth in biofuel use in the 2009–14 period, the vast majority of which will still be first-generation ethanol and biodiesel.[46]

Natural Gas Use Falls But Renaissance Is in the Pipeline

Saya Kitasei

Widespread economic contraction in 2009 caused the largest recorded annual decline in global natural gas consumption: a 2.1 percent drop to 103.8 trillion cubic feet (tcf).[1] (See Figure 1.) Gas consumption fell even more than coal and oil use did, reflecting the fact that energy consumption in North America and Europe—the largest gas consumers—fell sharply in response to the recession, while the world's fastest-growing energy market, China, used relatively little natural gas.[2] Overall, natural gas was responsible for 23.8 percent of global primary energy consumption in 2009, a slight decrease from 2008.[3] (See Figure 2.)

Yet the decline in gas use in 2009 will likely turn out to be a one-year anomaly, as a global renaissance in natural gas is beginning to take shape. Although global production of natural gas fell in response to reduced demand from 108.3 tcf in 2008 to 105.7 tcf in 2009, proven global reserves of natural gas rose 1.2 percent to an estimated 6,618 tcf.[4] (See Figure 3.) Potential recoverable reserves have been estimated at 16,200 tcf, which would be a 150-year supply at 2009 consumption rates—a figure that is expected to rise significantly as unconventional gas resources are discovered outside North America.[5]

In addition, the combination of growing supply and restrained demand led to a severe drop in spot natural gas prices in 2009 to less than half the record 2008 levels.[6] (See Figure 4.) These more moderate prices have increased natural gas' competitiveness with both oil and coal and have begun to spur demand in some countries.

The United States surpassed Russia in 2009 as the world's largest natural gas producer.[7] (See Figure 5.) With production increases from unconventional gas, especially from organic-rich shales where advanced well drilling and completion technologies have unlocked vast

new resources, U.S. production of natural gas rose to 20.9 tcf—up 3.5 percent from 2008 levels.[8] Since 1990, the share of total U.S. gas production attributable to unconventional gas,

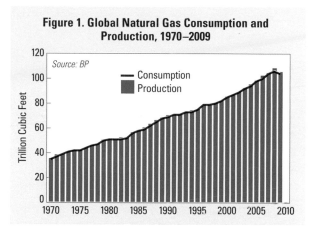

Figure 1. Global Natural Gas Consumption and Production, 1970–2009

Source: BP

— Consumption
▪ Production

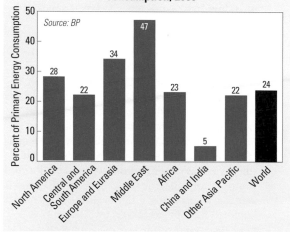

Figure 2. Natural Gas Share of Primary Energy Consumption, 2009

Source: BP

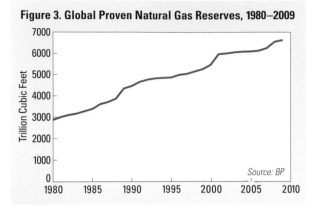

Figure 3. Global Proven Natural Gas Reserves, 1980–2009

Figure 4. Average Natural Gas Prices, Selected Indices, 1990–2009

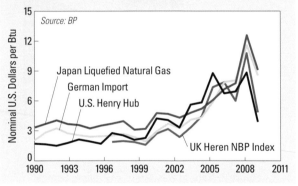

29 percent from their five-year lows in 2008 to 452 billion cubic feet, only about 11 percent of U.S. LNG import capacity was used.[13]

In Europe and Eurasia (the former Soviet Union states), the continuing effects of the recession contributed to a 6.8 percent decline in gas consumption since 2008, the largest drop of any region, for a total consumption of 37.4 tcf in 2009.[14] European pipeline gas prices, which are still mostly linked to the price of crude oil through long-term contracts, remained high relative to prices in North America, which are predominantly determined on spot markets.

The growing gap between contract prices and prices on Europe's fledgling spot markets led major European gas distributors to renegotiate contracts with Gazprom, the Russian gas giant that supplied 26.8 percent of Europe and Eurasia's gas during 2009.[15] Many analysts believe that the continuing transition away from oil-linked long-term contracts will quickly build momentum, changing the nature of global gas markets as well as long-term supply and demand trends in Europe.[16]

European countries continue to seek methods to diversify their gas supply and reduce their heavy dependence on Russia.[17] Major reserves of shale gas are thought to lie under Central and Eastern Europe, especially Poland, where several international and Polish gas companies began drilling during 2010.[18] Discussions continue about a group of new pipeline projects collectively known as the Southern Corridor, which would transport gas directly from the Caspian directly to Europe.[19] Russia has historically been the sole purchaser of Caspian gas, but the progress of Southern Corridor plans and the opening in December 2009 of a 1,139-mile pipeline from gas-rich Turkmenistan to China reveal that Russia's dominance of the European market is being reduced.[20]

Asia's consumption of gas grew by 3.4 percent overall, with declines in Japan, South Korea, Taiwan, Malaysia, and Hong Kong contrasting sharply with double-digit increases in developing economies such as Bangladesh and Indonesia.[21] The International Energy Agency

including tight sands, coal bed methane, and shale gas, has risen from 15 to 52 percent.[9] Estimates of technically recoverable natural gas in the United States reached 1,836 tcf in 2008—39 percent higher than assessments in 2006.[10]

Growth in domestic U.S. production helped keep gas prices on the largest U.S. spot market at an average of $4.85 per million Btu, significantly lower than in Europe and Asia.[11] As a result, despite a 1.5 percent fall in overall natural gas consumption, natural gas escaped the steeper losses experienced by oil and coal, consumption of which declined by 4.9 and 11.5 percent, respectively.[12] Lower prices also steered liquefied natural gas (LNG) away from U.S. markets, so that while U.S. LNG imports rose projects that Asia could overtake Europe as the second largest gas consumer by 2030.[22] Natural gas is making fast headway in India, where consumption grew by 25.9 percent to reach 5 billion cubic feet per day in 2009 and where the gas share of primary energy grew from 8.4 to 10.0 percent.[23] New policies promoting the use of natural gas, such as New Delhi's plans to replace coal-fired power plants, will drive future growth in India's natural gas consumption.[24]

China's gas consumption rose 9.4 percent to 2.8 tcf, as the country's voracious energy appetite escaped the brunt of the global recession.[25] China's large coal resource continues to provide most of the country's energy, with natural gas accounting for only 3.7 percent of China's primary energy consumption in 2009.[26] Demand is projected to grow rapidly, however, and China actively sought to secure new sources of natural gas during 2009.[27] In addition to the new Turkmenistan pipeline, China has invested in developing domestic natural gas projects, including in its coal bed methane and shale gas basins.[28]

With 40 percent of the world's proven natural gas reserves, which are found primarily in Qatar, Iran, and Saudi Arabia, the Middle East has the highest concentration of reserves.[29] (See Figure 6.) Positive economic performance and growth in the power sector and industrial demand in the region drove a 4.4 percent increase in consumption from 2008 to 2009 to reach 33.4 billion cubic feet per day, and this growth is predicted to increase.[30] The Middle East currently supplies approximately one fifth of world cross-border LNG trade, and it is expected to deliver over half of new LNG supply to 2015 and essentially all new global gas-to-liquids supply.[31] Nevertheless, most Middle Eastern natural gas is associated with oil, and some of it is still reinjected in order to enhance oil production instead of being sold.[32]

Africa accounts for only 3.2 percent of world gas consumption despite having 6.8 percent of the global production and 7.9 percent of proven reserves in 2009.[33] Both production and consumption decreased from 2008 levels, by 4.6 and 1.9 percent respectively.[34] The power sector is expected to drive demand growth in the

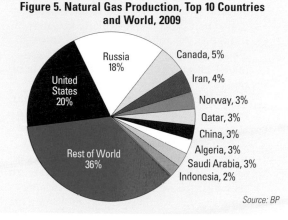

Figure 5. Natural Gas Production, Top 10 Countries and World, 2009

Source: BP

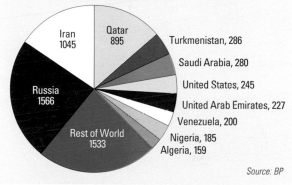

Figure 6. Proven Natural Gas Reserves, Top 10 Countries and World, Trillion Cubic Feet, 2009

Source: BP

future, but a lack of gas distribution infrastructure must be overcome: Nigeria alone flared an estimated 600 billion cubic feet of natural gas in 2007, enough to supply Norway and Poland combined, because the means to transport it to end-users did not exist.[35]

South American natural gas markets remained relatively isolated from the rest of the world during 2009, except for Trinidad and Tobago, which exported 696.8 billion cubic feet of liquefied natural gas, primarily to North America and Europe.[36] The region's production declined by 3.2 percent overall, while consumption declined by 4.2 percent.[37]

Pre-recession optimism in natural gas demand spurred a rapid build-out of liquefaction export capacity, particularly in Qatar, Indonesia, Australia, and Russia.[38] Although global liquefaction capacity reached an estimated 11 tcf/year in 2009, only 78 percent of that capacity was used.[39]

With an economic recovery and a growing resource base, last year's decline in natural gas consumption and production is likely to prove to be a brief hiatus in an otherwise upward trend. The emergence of unconventional gas means that supplies could be much greater than previously thought and spread across more countries and regions, possibly mitigating the concerns about energy security and price volatility that have prevented greater natural gas reliance to date. Growing global liquefaction capacity will contribute to building a more integrated global market for natural gas, further allowing regions to diversify their supplies.

Finally, growing interest in reducing carbon dioxide emissions in many regions could result in increased demand for natural gas. In 2008, natural gas accounted for 27.3 percent of primary fossil energy consumption but only some 20.6 percent of global carbon dioxide emissions from the consumption of energy—a gap driven by its low carbon content relative to oil and especially coal.[40] Its carbon advantages over coal, as well as its ability to back up variable renewable energy, have led many analysts to view natural gas as a potential transition fuel.[41] Several models predict that assigning a price on carbon, whether at the global or the national level, would promote natural gas consumption at the expense of coal, at least in the short run.[42]

World Nuclear Generation Stagnates

John Mulrow

For the second year in a row, global nuclear generating capacity has dropped slightly, reaching 370.9 gigawatts (GW) at the end of 2009.[1] (See Figure 1.) Just over 1 GW of capacity was added during the year, as India and Japan each connected a new plant to the grid.[2] At the same time, Japan closed two reactors and Lithuania one, so there were 2,506 megawatts (MW) worth of shutdowns.[3]

While installed capacity has been virtually flat for the past five years, construction starts surged in 2009 thanks to a burst of activity in China. (See Figure 2.) Altogether, construction began on 11 nuclear power reactors in 2009, the highest number since 14 units were started in 1985.[4] Some 56 nuclear reactors are now officially being built—but 13 of these have been "under construction" for more than 20 years, and 26 reactors have encountered "construction delays."[5]

As noted, 3 nuclear reactors were permanently closed in 2009, bringing the total number of decommissioned units to 126, representing a retired nuclear capacity of nearly 40 GW.[6] (See Figure 3.) The average age of all decommissioned reactors is 22 years.[7] Hamaoka 1 and 2, the two reactors that were shut down in Japan, were originally damaged by a 2007 earthquake that struck while they were undergoing safety-related upgrades.[8] The cost of seismic retrofitting of these two reactors was so high that the operator, Chubu Electric, decided to close them permanently and plans to build a single large reactor to replace them by 2018.[9]

In the United States, in early 2010 the Obama administration asked Congress to expand the existing nuclear loan-guarantee program from $18 billion to $54 billion in an effort to use federal subsidies to spur the first U.S. reactor construction starts in more than three decades.[10]

The expense of the required subsidies has soared, as has the capital cost of erecting a nuclear power plant—which is now more than six times that of a gas combined-cycle plant.[11] The first two reactors granted federal loan guarantees by the U.S. administration have an eye-popping price tag of $14 billion, well over the

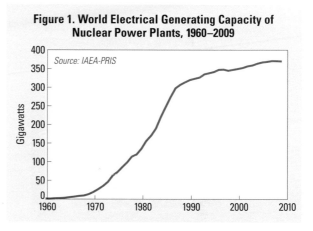

Figure 1. World Electrical Generating Capacity of Nuclear Power Plants, 1960–2009

Source: IAEA-PRIS

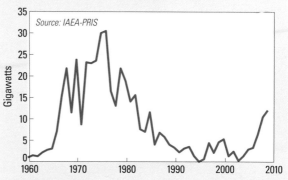

Figure 2. World Nuclear Reactor Construction Starts, 1960–2009

Source: IAEA-PRIS

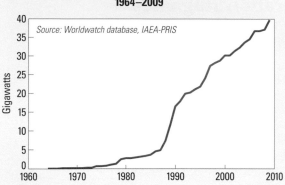

Figure 3. Nuclear Capacity of Decommissioned Plants, 1964–2009

Source: Worldwatch database, IAEA-PRIS

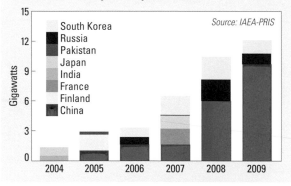

Figure 4. Nuclear Power Construction Initiations by Country, 2004–2009

Source: IAEA-PRIS

South Korea
Russia
Pakistan
Japan
India
France
Finland
China

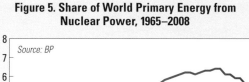

Figure 5. Share of World Primary Energy from Nuclear Power, 1965–2008

Source: BP

$8.4 billion guarantee they are slated to receive.[12] As a result, it is not yet certain that these two reactors will actually be built, and the total proposed loan guarantees of $54 billion would only support 7–10 new reactors according to the U.S. Department of Energy.[13]

Added capacity in China, India, and Japan accounted for 80 percent of new grid-connected nuclear energy in the past five years.[14] Only two other countries have added new nuclear capacity in that period: South Korea and Romania each brought one reactor online.[15] One significant difference between the reactors added in Asia and those in Europe is the plant construction time. The 4 reactors added in Romania, Russia, and the Ukraine most recently took 18–24 years to build, while the 10 reactors that went online in China, India, Japan, and South Korea took on average 5 years each.[16]

Nuclear construction starts in China have shot up in the last five years, going from a single 1 GW reactor start in 2005 to nine starts totaling 9.7 GW of planned capacity in 2009.[17] China has accounted for more than half the global construction starts in the past two years.[18] (See Figure 4.)

Interest in nuclear power is growing in the Middle East—from Egypt to Iran—where electricity demand is booming. In late 2009, the United Arab Emirates (UAE) placed an order for 5.6 GW of nuclear capacity from a major South Korean supplier.[19] However, the UAE and its neighbors currently lack the skills or institutions to effectively operate and regulate the nuclear industry, and it remains to be seen how successful these efforts will be.

In 2008, nuclear power's share of the world's commercial primary energy continued its downward trend, falling to 5.5 percent, compared with a peak of 6.4 percent in 2001 and 2002.[20] (See Figure 5.) Some 13.5 percent of the world's electricity was supplied by nuclear in 2008, down from 16.8 percent in 2000.[21] Of the 31 countries that count on nuclear reactors for a portion of their primary energy, only 4 countries increased the share of electricity supplied by nuclear power in 2008.[22]

Even the recent stepped-up pace of construction is not yet sufficient to maintain, let alone significantly increase, nuclear power's share of global electricity, since the average currently operating reactor is already 25 years old and the fleet will face accelerated shutdowns after 2020.[23] It is estimated that just to keep nuclear generation at current levels by 2015, the industry will need to complete all 52 reactors currently under construction and add another 16,000 megawatts of capacity over the next five years.[24]

That scale of nuclear revival appears improbable. The considerable barriers to adding new nuclear capacity include high costs, the need to build specialized industrial capacity that does not currently exist in most countries, stringent safety regulations that must now be adapted to a new generation of reactors, and a shortage of trained workers to run and maintain nuclear power plants. A large share of the nuclear work force in Europe and North America is rapidly approaching retirement age.[25]

John Mulrow was a MAP Sustainable Energy Fellow at Worldwatch Institute in 2009-10.

Wind Power Growth Continues to Break Records Despite Recession

Saya Kitasei

Global wind power capacity increased by 38,343 megawatts to a total of 158,505 megawatts in 2009.[1] Despite a widespread economic recession, new wind power capacity grew more than 31 percent in cumulative installations, the highest rate in the last eight years.[2] (See Figures 1 and 2.) Worldwide, wind power contributed 340 billion kilowatt-hours, or 2 percent, to global electricity consumption in 2009.[3]

The Asian market became the main driver behind the wind industry's continued growth, with 15,442 megawatts of new wind capacity installed in 2009, which increased Asia's total installed capacity by 64 percent over 2008.[4] (See Figure 3.) China passed the United States to become the world's largest wind turbine market, installing 13,803 megawatts in 2009 to reach a total of 25,805 megawatts.[5] China accounted for more than one third of the world's wind capacity installations in 2009, more than doubling its cumulative installed capacity for the fourth year in a row.[6] The country continued to pursue an aggressive policy agenda for renewables, introducing a fixed feed-in tariff for new onshore wind power plants and outspending the United States on renewable energy.[7] Nevertheless, China continues to suffer from inadequate transmission capacity; as a result, over a quarter of its existing wind capacity is not connected to the grid.[8]

India installed 2,459 megawatts of new capacity last year, consolidating its position as the fifth largest wind energy producer in the world.[9] Both India and China have strong domestic wind turbine manufacturing industries with large market shares in Asia: 4 of the top 10 wind turbine manufacturers by market share in 2009 were Chinese or Indian, together serving 29 percent of the world market.[10] (See Figure 4.)

The United States maintained its global lead in total installed capacity.[11] (See Figure 5.) U.S. capacity increased by 10,010 megawatts, or 40 percent, to a total of 35,086 megawatts.[12] Thanks to this, wind power accounted for 42 percent of new installed power capacity in the United States, passing natural gas and assuming first place.[13] Last year's strong growth partially

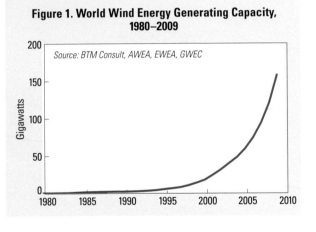

Figure 1. World Wind Energy Generating Capacity, 1980–2009

Source: BTM Consult, AWEA, EWEA, GWEC

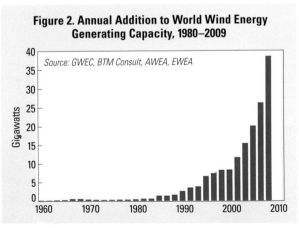

Figure 2. Annual Addition to World Wind Energy Generating Capacity, 1980–2009

Source: GWEC, BTM Consult, AWEA, EWEA

reflects a backlog of turbines ordered in 2008 and delayed in anticipation of an extension of the federal Production Tax Credit, which was finally passed in early 2009 as part of the Recovery Act.[14] Canada installed 950 megawatts of new wind capacity, increasing its total installed capacity 40 percent.[15]

In the United States, Texas again installed more new wind capacity than any other state, bringing its total installed wind capacity to 9,410 megawatts.[16] Other leading states include Iowa, with a total wind capacity of 3,670 megawatts, and California, with 2,794 megawatts.[17] Indiana installed 905 megawatts in 2009, more than any state but Texas.[18]

Altogether, the 27 countries of the European Union installed 10,163 megawatts of wind power in 2009.[19] For the second year running, wind represented more capacity additions than any other electricity source in Europe, accounting for 39 percent of new installations.[20] Germany installed 1,917 megawatts in 2009, which put it narrowly behind China to have the third largest total capacity of wind power in the world.[21] Germany's end-of-year wind capacity, approaching 25,780 megawatts, was only 8 percent higher than in 2008, continuing the country's trend of slowing growth.[22]

Spain passed Germany to lead Europe in new wind power installations. Some 2,459 megawatts of additional capacity brought Spain's total to 19,149 megawatts, putting the country on track to surpass a 2005 government target of 20,000 megawatts of wind power capacity by 2010.[23] Generation from wind power reached 36,188,000 megawatt-hours, or 14 percent of Spain's total electricity generation in 2009, overtaking coal for the first time.[24] On December 30th, wind power set a new record in Spain, reaching demand coverage of 54 percent.[25]

The rest of Europe installed 363 megawatts, bringing Europe's total wind capacity to 76,152 megawatts, or 48 percent of global capacity.[26] Italy, France, and the United Kingdom installed 1,114 megawatts, 1,088 megawatts, and 1,077 megawatts of new wind capacity, respectively.[27] Turkey installed 343 megawatts of new capacity,

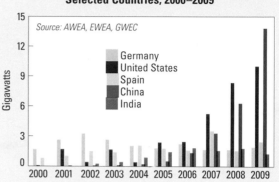

Figure 3. Annual Wind Energy Capacity Additions, Selected Countries, 2000–2009

Source: AWEA, EWEA, GWEC

Germany
United States
Spain
China
India

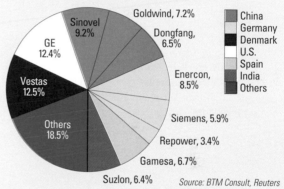

Figure 4. Top 10 Wind Turbine Manufacturers by Global Market Share, 2009

Sinovel 9.2%
GE 12.4%
Vestas 12.5%
Others 18.5%
Goldwind, 7.2%
Dongfang, 6.5%
Enercon, 8.5%
Siemens, 5.9%
Repower, 3.4%
Gamesa, 6.7%
Suzlon, 6.4%

China
Germany
Denmark
U.S.
Spain
India
Others

Source: BTM Consult, Reuters

increasing its total wind capacity 75 percent.[28] Denmark continues to have the highest share of wind in its electricity supply in the world, with wind meeting 20 percent of demand.[29]

Elsewhere, wind power continued to make inroads, and commercial installations can now be found in at least 82 countries.[30] Australia added 383 megawatts, increasing its installed wind capacity 26 percent to a total of 1,877 megawatts.[31] Mexico's wind capacity grew by over 137 percent in 2009, faster than any other country.[32] It was followed by China, Turkey, Morocco, and Brazil, demonstrating that wind power is beginning to gain momentum in the

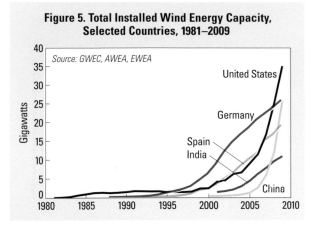

Figure 5. Total Installed Wind Energy Capacity, Selected Countries, 1981–2009

Source: GWEC, AWEA, EWEA

developing world.[33] Africa continued to trail, with only 0.5 percent of total global capacity, although Egypt and Morocco installed a combined 169 megawatts of capacity in 2009.[34]

Offshore wind capacity constitutes only a fraction of total wind capacity, but it continued to rise in 2009, with 689 megawatts added worldwide.[35] In Europe, 577 megawatts were installed, an increase of 54 percent over 2008 installations, bringing offshore capacity to 2,056 megawatts, or just under 3 percent of Europe's

total wind capacity.[36] The United Kingdom remained the world leader in offshore wind, with 883 megawatts of total installed capacity.[37] Germany's North Sea waters promise to be a major growth area for offshore wind, with 1,040 megawatts of capacity under construction and an additional 8,589 megawatts approved.[38] China, the first country outside of Europe to install an offshore wind farm, built 21 megawatts of new offshore capacity in 2009.[39] These new additions are part of the 100-megawatt Shanghai East Bridge Offshore Wind Farm, slated to be completed by May 2010.[40]

Despite a tough financial year, investment in new wind energy capacity increased by 33 percent in 2009, to $63 billion.[41] Worldwide, the wind industry provided some 550,000 direct and indirect jobs, up 37.5 percent from 2008.[42] The World Wind Energy Association predicts that these jobs, which are primarily highly skilled ones, will reach 1 million by 2012.[43] BTM Consult, a Danish consulting firm, projects that total global wind capacity will reach 447,000 megawatts in the next five years and about 1 million megawatts by the end of 2019, meeting 8.4 percent of global electricity demand.[44]

Record Growth in Photovoltaic Capacity and Momentum Builds for Concentrating Solar Power

James Russell

An estimated 7,300 megawatts (MW) of new solar photovoltaic (PV) power capacity was installed in 2009—20 percent more than was added in 2008.[1] With this record addition, global installed PV capacity surpassed 21,000 megawatts, producing enough power to satisfy the annual electricity use of about 5.5 million households.[2] In addition, 127 MW of solar thermal electric power plants came online in 2009, bringing the total operating capacity of such plants to 613 MW.[3] Solar energy harnessed by PV and thermal electric plants now meets about 1 percent of electricity demand in Germany and more than 2 percent of demand in Spain.[4]

Europe continues to be the center of global PV demand, installing 5,280 MW in 2009, equal to 72 percent of the global total.[5] (See Figure 1.) Germany alone was responsible for more than half of global PV installation, with a total of 3,800 MW installed.[6] Much of this record capacity increase was completed only in December, as solar developers rushed to complete projects before Germany's feed-in tariff was reduced by 10 percent in January 2010.[7] Installations by the previous record holder, Spain, plummeted from 2,700 MW in 2008 to about 70 MW in 2009.[8] This decline came as no surprise, however, as Spanish policymakers sharply reduced the solar feed-in-tariff and introduced a new project approval process to control costs and project quality.[9]

Italy was the second largest market for PV, with 580 MW installed.[10] Japan took third place with 480 MW installed, spurred on by a new obligation for utilities to purchase surplus PV electricity.[11] The United States was the fourth largest market, with about 470 MW installed, and the Czech Republic was fifth, with 410 MW installed.[12]

In 2009, the installation of solar thermal electric plants, also known as concentrating solar power (CSP), was focused in Spain, where 120 MW was added and the current goal is to reach 500 MW of installed capacity.[13] CSP plants as large as 50 MW are eligible for Spain's feed-in tariff. Historically, the United States has been the leader of CSP development, with about 430 MW operating at the end of 2009.[14] But only 7 MW of new CSP capacity was installed there in 2009 and just a total of 77 MW since 2000.[15] Yet both Spain and the United States appear committed to substantial CSP growth in the near term. Spain's CSP industry association expects an additional 900 MW of CSP plants to be operational or under construction in 2010.[16] Utilities in California signed agreements in 2008 and 2009 for more than 3,000 MW of CSP, though much of this awaits regulatory approval.[17]

Concentrating solar power differs from photovoltaic cells in both the technology used and the opportunities presented. CSP uses the sun's energy to generate steam that drives a turbine and turns an electrical generator. One advantage of CSP is that a facility can store some of the

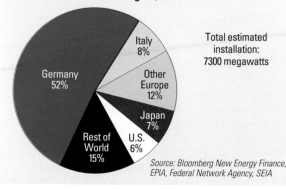

Figure 1. Share of Global PV Installation by Country or Region, 2009

Total estimated installation: 7300 megawatts

Germany 52%
Italy 8%
Other Europe 12%
Japan 7%
U.S. 6%
Rest of World 15%

Source: Bloomberg New Energy Finance, EPIA, Federal Network Agency, SEIA

thermal energy collected and then use that stored energy to operate even when the sun is not shining. Spain's 50-MW Andasol-1 includes thermal storage that allows the plant to operate at full load for 7.5 hours without sun.[18] CSP also allows hybridization with fossil fuel power plants. For example, the Martin integrated solar combined cycle plant nearing completion in Florida will add 75 MW of solar thermal electric capacity to an existing combined-cycle gas power plant.[19]

Though solar photovoltaic cells are typically deployed in smaller increments than CSP, overall PV capacity additions have greatly outpaced those of CSP in recent years, and the manufacture of cells has grown rapidly. Global production of photovoltaic cells increased by about 3,600 MW in 2009, reaching 10,660 MW.[20] (See Figure 2.) The 10 largest manufacturers produced about 5,450 MW, just over half of the total.[21] First Solar was at the front of this group, becoming the first company to produce more than 1,000 MW in a single year.[22]

Companies based in China or Taiwan accounted for 49 percent of cell production, up from just 26 percent in 2008.[23] (See Figure 3.) European companies produced 18 percent of cells, Japanese companies 14 percent, and U.S. companies 6 percent.[24] However, with major manufacturers listing on international stock exchanges and building plants overseas to take advantage of lower production costs or government incentives, both ownership and production of many firms crosses national boundaries. For example, two solar companies based in China and one from Japan were among the 45 solar companies awarded $860 million in tax credits under the 2009 Recovery Act to open or expand clean tech manufacturing facilities in the United States.[25]

At present the PV market features a diverse set of technologies. Major producers offer monocrystalline silicon-wafer-based PV cells that convert the sun's radiation to electricity with an efficiency of more than 19 percent and thin-film cells with efficiencies of around 10 percent.[26] For the five years ending in 2008, the production of thin-film photovoltaic cells grew at a much faster rate than silicon-wafer-based cells, albeit from a much smaller base.[27] Some industry analysts have predicted that this pattern will continue, with thin-film cells more than doubling their market share from 14 percent in 2008 to 31 percent in 2013.[28] Indeed, thin film continued its advance in 2009 to reach 19 percent of cell production, led by First Solar's production growth of more than 500 MW.[29]

This change in market share is primarily due to the lower cost per watt offered by thin-film PV cells. Fast demand growth from the European market coupled with a tight supply of polysilicon caused average PV module prices, across all technologies, to rise from $3 per watt in 2003 to a peak of about $4 per watt in 2007, in spite of improvements in manufacturing and the rapid growth of production in China.[30] In this environment, producers of thin-film modules, which use little or no polysilicon, had a cost advantage and rapidly scaled up production.

Module prices declined only slightly in 2008, but in 2009 the price outlook for PV shifted significantly downward. The polysilicon shortage eased in 2008 as new production came online, and demand growth was then curbed by the reining in of the Spanish market and the global financial crisis.[31] With continued growth of supply, the average price of polysilicon wafer-based modules is estimated to have dropped 38 percent relative to 2008, and estimates of the 2010 price declined from $2.45 in early 2009 to just $1.60 later that year.[32] Declining PV costs will encourage PV deployment in the years ahead, but in the short term the availability of low-cost, polysilicon wafer-based modules with greater efficiency may erode the cost advantage of the thin-film technology and slow its growth.

Feed-in tariffs are the principal policy tool supporting Europe's preeminence in solar installations. The general principle of a feed-in-tariff is to subsidize the installation of renewable energy by establishing a guaranteed price over a fixed period for the electricity produced by a renewable energy source, such as solar PV. As the cost of installations declines, feed-in tariffs are similarly reduced to ensure that developers are not overcompensated.[33] Germany, Italy, and the Czech Republic are now lowering these tariffs to reflect the declining price of modules.[34]

The popularity of this type of subsidy is on the rise.[35] Both the United Kingdom and Greece recently introduced new feed-in tariffs for PV systems, as did Ontario (Canada) and Taiwan.[36] Malaysia plans to introduce one soon.[37] Many state governments in the United States are also considering feed-in tariffs as a possible complement to the dozens of renewable portfolio standards, net metering programs, and investment subsidies that currently encourage solar power.[38] But opinion on the benefits of such an approach is not uniform: South Korea has signaled that its feed-in tariff, which expires in 2012, may be replaced by a renewable portfolio standard requiring energy companies to get a specific share of their electricity supply from renewables.[39]

Though in 2009 Europe maintained the large lead in solar power deployment that it has held since 2005, the year also brought some hints of possible changes to come. Japan signaled its commitment to return to leadership of PV deployment, with a vision of increasing PV capacity to 28,000 MW by 2020.[40] In India, the cabinet approved the Jawaharlal Nehru National Solar Mission. Noting both the environmental and energy security challenges faced by India and the country's vast solar energy potential, the Solar Mission has a three-phase plan for installing 20,000 MW of solar power capacity by 2022.[41] And in 2009 China strengthened its renewable energy law, introduced a subsidy of 50 percent for certain solar demonstration projects and of 20 yuan (about $2.90) per watt for building-integrated PV, and increased the target for solar power capacity from 1,800 MW to 20,000 MW in 2020.[42] India and China plan to use both PV and CSP to achieve their new goals.

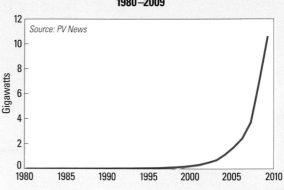

Figure 2. Annual Global Production of Photovoltaic Cells, 1980–2009

Source: PV News

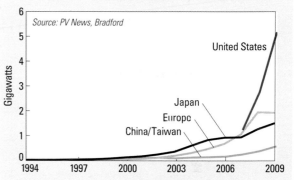

Figure 3. Photovoltaic Production by Country or Region, 1994–2009

Source: PV News, Bradford

Meeting just these three countries' goals will require quadrupling the current global solar capacity.[43] The solar industry appears eager for the challenge, with two companies already announcing agreements with Chinese partners to build 2,000 MW of PV and 2,000 MW of CSP.[44]

James Russell is an environmental engineer and a researcher at the Asia Pacific Energy Research Centre.

Auto Industry in Turmoil
But Chinese Production Surges

Michael Renner

The year 2009 was one of deep crisis for large parts of the world's automobile industry, with production and sales that plunged in many countries, factory closings, job loss, and a reshuffling of the leading producers. Production of passenger cars and light trucks declined 13 percent, from 68.2 million units in 2008 to 59.2 million, according to the London-based IHS

Global Insight Automotive Group.[1] (See Figure 1.) The historic peak was 69 million vehicles in 2007.[2] Sales dropped a less precipitous but still significant 6 percent, from 66.2 million light vehicles in 2008 (and the previous peak of 69.4 million in 2007) to 62.4 million in 2009.[3]

North America, Japan, and Western Europe have long been the industry's dominant powers. But China is now the most dynamic force. Having overtaken Germany in 2006, and then the United States in 2008, China also breezed past Japan in 2009 to become the world's largest automobile producer.[4]

China's output soared from 8.6 million passenger vehicles in 2008 to 12.5 million in 2009.[5] (See Table 1 and Figure 2.) Japan's output declined from 11.1 million to 7.7 million.[6] The United States saw a massive reduction, from 8.5 million vehicles to 5.6 million, and Germany— the fourth-largest producer—registered a less dramatic drop, from 5.8 million to 5.1 million units.[7] Brazil and India were the only other leading producer nations where car manufacturing rose in 2009. Brazil's output rose from 2.9 million to 3.0 million; India's went from 2.1 million to 2.3 million.[8]

At least 39 countries produce cars, according to the International Organization of Motor Vehicle Manufacturers.[9] One third of them each produced at least 1 million vehicles annually.[10] But the top four together accounted for 52 percent of global output, and the top 10 produce 76 percent.[11]

There is far more production capacity in the world than is needed. The portion of facilities actually in use dropped from 83 percent in 2007 to just 65 percent in 2009.[12] The active share is lowest in the Middle East and Africa (51 percent) and in Eastern Europe (39 percent).[13] Such leading producers as China, Japan, Ger-

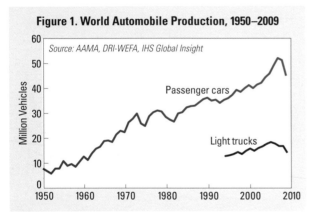

Figure 1. World Automobile Production, 1950–2009

Source: AAMA, DRI-WEFA, IHS Global Insight

Passenger cars

Light trucks

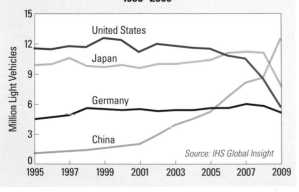

Figure 2. Light Vehicle Production, Leading Countries, 1995–2009

United States

Japan

Germany

China

Source: IHS Global Insight

many, South Korea, and Brazil managed to keep more than 70 percent of their facilities in operation throughout 2009, but in the United States the figure was just 57 percent.[14]

Except for the Hyundai-Kia group, all leading manufacturers suffered a drop in light-vehicle assembly between 2007 and 2009. Despite a reduction from 10.1 million to 7.7 million, the Toyota group remained the largest car company.[15] General Motors saw its output plunge from 9.3 million to 6.4 million, as the company entered bankruptcy and underwent drastic restructuring measures.[16] The other companies in the top 10 are Volkswagen-Porsche, Ford, Renault-Nissan, Hyundai, Fiat, Honda, and PSA (Peugeot).[17]

Driven by government incentives that reduced the sales tax on fuel-efficient vehicles, Chinese sales surged by more than 40 percent in 2009 to reach 7.3 million cars.[18] This was up from an average of just 2.6 million in 2001–07.[19] (Including trucks and buses, 2009 sales added up to 13 million vehicles, making China the world's largest national motor vehicle market—ahead of the United States.)[20]

Car purchases in Brazil and India also rose to new levels. India recorded an increase from an average of 800,000 in 2001–07 to 1.4 million in 2009; Brazil went from 1.4 million to 2.5 million.[21] But the West European new-car market shrunk from an annual average of 14.6 million vehicles sold in 2001–07 to 13.4 million in 2009.[22] Japanese sales of about 4 million passenger cars were down from 4.8 million in 2004 and a historic peak of 5.1 million in 1990.[23]

The United States saw the most pronounced drop in car purchases. In 2009, sales there declined 21 percent, to 10.3 million cars and light trucks.[24] This is the lowest figure since 1982 and is down from 16.7 million in 2001–07.[25] And according to the Earth Policy Institute, an estimated 14 million old cars were scrapped in 2009, the first time since World War II that discards exceeded sales.[26] The U.S. vehicle fleet thus shrank from 250 million to 246 million.[27]

A number of countries—including the United States, Germany, France, Spain, Italy, and the

Table 1. Light Vehicle Production, Leading Countries, 1995–2009

	United States	Japan	Germany	China
	(million light vehicles)			
1995	11.6	9.9	4.5	1.1
1996	11.5	10.0	4.7	1.2
1997	11.8	10.6	4.9	1.3
1998	11.7	9.8	5.6	1.4
1999	12.6	9.7	5.5	1.6
2000	12.4	9.9	5.4	1.8
2001	11.2	9.6	5.5	2.0
2002	12.0	10.0	5.3	2.9
2003	11.8	10.0	5.4	3.9
2004	11.6	10.2	5.4	4.5
2005	11.5	10.4	5.6	5.2
2006	10.8	11.1	5.6	6.7
2007	10.5	11.2	6.0	8.1
2008	8.5	11.1	5.8	8.6
2009	5.6	7.7	5.1	12.5

Source: Colin Couchman, IHS Global Insight Automotive Group, London, e-mail to author, 13 January 2010.

United Kingdom—adopted incentives in 2009 for scrapping old vehicles and replacing them with new models. Claims of environmental benefits (getting the most inefficient vehicles off the roads) notwithstanding, the prime motivation was to give the auto industry a shot in the arm.[28] Some of the incentives are expiring in 2010; sales in Europe, for instance, might shrink by as many as 2 million vehicles as a result.[29]

In China, by contrast, the incentives to scrap older vehicles will be increased more than threefold, reaching the equivalent of about $2,600 per car.[30] This is expected to increase sales to almost 9 million in 2010.[31] Similarly, 2010 sales gains are anticipated in Russia, where the government, in reaction to the 2009 sales slump, decided to pay about $1,660 to buyers of new domestic-made cars who replace vehicles that are at least 10 years old.[32]

Although market saturation is increasingly characteristic of the mature western markets, the rapid growth in emerging markets is nonetheless driving the continued expansion of the global automobile fleet. The number of passenger cars on the world's roads has risen from 413 million in 1992 to 642 million in 2009.[33] Global Insight predicts a further rise to 670 million by the end of 2011.[34] Including not just passenger cars but also light-duty and heavy-duty trucks, the fleet numbers have risen from 559 million to 916 million over the same period of time and may reach 959 million by 2011.[35] (See Figure 3.)

Concerns about energy import dependence, oil prices, and environmental impacts have led to a growing desire to find suitable replacements for internal combustion engines. So-called hybrid vehicles (using an electric motor alongside a conventional engine) and fully electric vehicles are receiving growing attention. Toyota, Honda, Nissan, GM, Ford, Audi, BMW, Fiat, and BYD have all announced plans to introduce hybrids and electrics.[36] But forecasts of future global production of such vehicles diverge widely.

PricewaterhouseCoopers projects that production of gasoline-electric hybrids worldwide will grow from about 900,000 in 2009 to some 3.3 million by 2015.[37] The number of diesel-electric hybrids might grow from less than 4,000

to more than 300,000, and fully electric vehicles from about 6,000 to 415,000.[38] The combined share of such alternative models might thus grow from 0.7 percent today to 3.7 percent of total car production.[39] The Boston Consulting Group, meanwhile, forecasts a market share of 26 percent for hybrids and fully electric models of new car sales in 2020 in China, Japan, the United States, and Western Europe—which would mean approximately 14 million cars.[40]

In the United States, hybrid sales in 2009 came to about 290,000, or about 2.8 percent of total sales.[41] Even though absolute sales numbers declined from the previous year, this is nonetheless the highest share ever, since sales of conventional models dropped far more.[42] In Japan, Toyota's Prius hybrid became the best-selling model, with close to 209,000 vehicles bought in 2009—almost triple the 2008 sales.[43]

A recent U.S. study suggests that a car running on electricity would reduce emissions of volatile organic compounds by 93 percent and nitrogen oxide emissions by 31 percent compared with a gasoline-powered car.[44] But a December 2009 report from the U.S. National Research Council (NRC) cautioned that plug-in electrics will not emit less carbon dioxide than hybrids unless the bulk of electricity is generated without burning fossil fuels.[45]

The NRC report also found that the high costs of plug-in electric cars were unlikely to drop much in the near future without a fundamental breakthrough in battery technology.[46] For several decades, higher manufacturing costs will more than offset the lower per-mile driving costs that plug-ins offer compared with conventional vehicles. The study concluded that, realistically, no more than 13 million plug-in vehicles will be on U.S. roads by 2030.[47] Without technology breakthroughs, the future of plug-ins in other countries may be similarly limited.

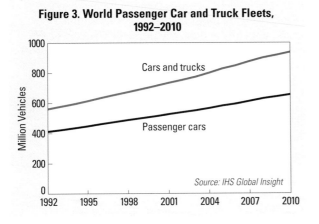

Figure 3. World Passenger Car and Truck Fleets, 1992–2010

Source: IHS Global Insight

Air Travel Trends Mixed as Carbon Footprint Grows

Nausheen Khan and Kelsey Russell

In 2008, the latest year with available data, the traveling public flew 4.28 trillion passenger-kilometers on airplanes, a 1.3 percent increase from 2007.[1] (See Figure 1.) The distance that passengers travel has increased every year except 1991 and 2001 since statistics were first recorded by the International Civil Aviation Organization (ICAO) in the 1940s.[2] In the past two decades, the number of passenger-kilometers traveled more than doubled—from 1.7 trillion in 1988 to 4.3 trillion in 2008.[3]

Passenger-kilometers are calculated by multiplying the distance of a trip by the number of passengers traveling.[4] ICAO uses passenger-kilometers to monitor air traffic because it captures both the number of travelers and the distance traveled, which is a clearer indicator of travel trends than passenger numbers alone.

In 2008, due to the global recession, the air transport industry experienced the slowest rate of growth since 2002, measured in terms of passenger-kilometers.[5] This lagging growth rate likely continued in 2009, with a 2 percent decline.[6] However, ICAO predicts that as the global economy revives, air travel in 2010 will continue the growth trend seen prior to the recession, with an expected growth rate of 6.4 percent over 2009.[7]

In North American markets, the number of passenger-kilometers traveled in 2008 increased by 3.8 percent from the previous year, reaching 1,386 billion.[8] Asia and the Pacific region had no growth and remained at 1,150 billion passenger-kilometers, while Europe had an increase of 4.1 percent to reach 1,221 billion passenger-kilometers.[9] The number of passenger-kilometers in the Middle East increased by 7.5 percent, to 233 billion, and Latin America and the Caribbean had a growth rate of 10.3 percent—the highest of any region—to 190

billion passenger-kilometers.[10]

Although passenger-kilometers increased in 2008, the number of people traveling by air actually declined by 0.4 percent from 2007, down to 2,271 million passengers.[11] (See Figure 2.) The slight decline in the number of passengers—one of the few years this has happened in the past six decades—can be attributed to

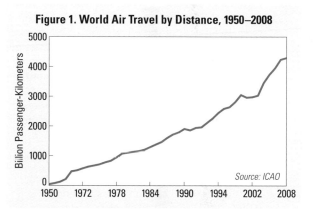

Figure 1. World Air Travel by Distance, 1950–2008

Source: ICAO

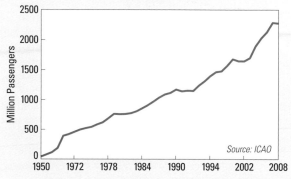

Figure 2. World Passenger Air Travel by Volume, 1950–2008

Source: ICAO

the global financial crisis and the downturn in the economy.[12]

Global air carriers posted an aggregated operating loss of $8.9 billion in 2008, a dramatic departure from the $19.9 billion profit of 2007.[13] Even in 2009 airlines had not recovered, although operating losses were about half the figure of 2008 and stood at $4.1 billion.[14] During this time oil prices were quite volatile and fell from a high of $137 per barrel in July 2008 to a low of $43 in December 2008, which affected airline fuel costs—a significant expense for airline carriers.[15]

As the number of miles flown increases, so does the pollution from flying. Greenhouse gas emissions from air travel account for an estimated 2–3 percent of global human-made emissions each year.[16] Carbon dioxide (CO_2) is the most significant of these emissions. The average amount of CO_2 released during a flight varies by distance. As more emissions are released during takeoff or landing than during flights at a cruising altitude, longer flights emit less CO_2 per kilometer than shorter ones do. For short-haul flights of less than 483 kilometers, on average 0.19 kilograms (kg) of CO_2 are released per passenger-kilometer; for medium-haul flights of less than 1,126 kilometers, the figure is 0.10 kg of CO_2 per passenger kilometer; and for long-haul flights of 1,126 kilometers or more, it is 0.09 kg of CO_2.[17] Other modes of transportation have varying effects on the climate, with buses emitting less CO_2 per passenger-kilometer than subways and commuter rail do.[18] (See Table 1.)

The proportion of national CO_2 emissions attributable to plane travel is higher in many industrial countries than in developing ones, and emissions from aviation are increasing faster in industrial countries than those from any other sector.[19] A U.N. Framework Convention on Climate Change report in 2007 highlighted the fact that greenhouse gas emissions from fuels sold for use in international aviation increased by 65.8 percent between 1990 and 2005.[20]

Other emissions during air travel also affect climate change. Water vapor, a by-product of fuel combustion, accelerates the formation of

Table 1. Carbon Emissions for Different Modes of Transport

Mode	Kilograms CO_2 per Passenger-Kilometer
Airplane	0.09–0.19
Bus	0.17
Subway (Metro)	0.26
U.S. Commuter Rail	0.30

Source: T. Damassa, Carbon Dioxide (CO_2) Inventory Report for Calendar Year 2008 *(Washington, DC: World Resources Institute, 2010).*

contrails—the white streaks in the sky often seen behind an airplane—when combined with carbon dioxide and nitrogen oxide.[21] Contrails raise global temperatures by reflecting heat back to Earth, most significantly through the development of ice-laden cirrus clouds. [22] According to the Intergovernmental Panel on Climate Change, the water vapor in contrails is about two to four times more effective than CO_2 at trapping heat in Earth's atmosphere.[23]

The European Union's (EU) Emission Trading Scheme (ETS) will include international aviation by January 2012, even though this was not explicitly included in the Kyoto Protocol on climate change.[24] This will limit the greenhouse gas emissions from any airline flying within the EU or into or out of the region. So it affects not only domestic airlines but also those operating outside the EU. Those that go over the ETS limits will pay a fine. The Chinese aviation industry, for example, could pay a total of 17.6 billion yuan (some $2.6 billion) in carbon levies to the EU between 2012 and 2020, based on the expected travel of Chinese airplanes to and from Europe.[25] The EU reports that by 2020, approximately 183 million tons of CO_2 will be saved per year on the flights included in the ETS.[26] This represents a 46 percent reduction from the level predicted by current trends if the scheme were not adopted.[27]

In 2005, the United Kingdom began a "sustainable aviation" program to reduce pollution, improve fuel efficiency, and include aircraft emissions in EU carbon trading.[28] Aviation emissions there accounted for 6 percent of national CO_2 emissions in 2006 but are predicted to increase to 25 percent by 2030.[29] In 2008, the United Kingdom introduced the Climate Change Act, the world's first legally binding carbon framework (which includes emissions from air travel) to reduce greenhouse gas emissions by 80 percent from 1990 levels by 2050.[30] In a move that further shows the nation's willingness to address problems with air travel, in May 2010 Prime Minister David Cameron cancelled plans to build additional runways at Heathrow, Gatwick, and Stansted airports.[31]

Many researchers and airlines are looking for technological solutions to help mitigate the environmental effects of global air travel. In 2008, Virgin Atlantic became the first airline to use low-carbon jet fuel, a 20 percent biofuel mix of babassu and coconut oil, in its Boeing 747-400 flight from London to Amsterdam.[32] As of May 2010, at least seven commercial airlines have flown aircraft powered with biofuel–jet fuel blends in their engines.[33] British Airways (BA) is working with the Solena Group, a bioenergy and biofuels company, to launch Europe's first plant for sustainable jet fuels made from food and plant waste.[34] As of 2014, several BA aircraft will operate using low-carbon fuel. As a result of the plant, BA expects that approximately 550,000 tons of CO_2 emissions will be avoided per year, a 95 percent savings over jet fuel from fossil fuels.[35]

After suffering significant losses in 2009 due to the global recession, the airline industry is finally recovering—but at the expense of passengers. In the first quarter of 2010, airfares increased by 5 percent and customers were faced with unexpected charges.[36] Many airlines have offset their losses by offering fewer flights and charging customers fees for carry-on bags, aisle seats, meals, and even pillows.[37] At the same time, the International Air Transport Association released the Automated Carrier Baggage Rules, providing consumers and airlines with a central database of uniform baggage rules.[38] These not only help passengers, they also let airlines streamline the costs and time associated with handling baggage.[39] A few advances have also been made to protect passenger rights: the European Court of Justice in 2009 issued a judgment on European passenger rights legislation that entitles passengers to monetary compensation for flights that reach their destination three hours after the originally scheduled arrival time.[40]

Nausheen Khan and Kelsey Russell were interns at Worldwatch Institute.

Environment and Climate Trends

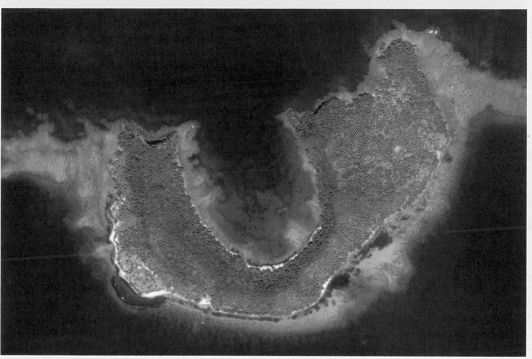

Matangi Island, Fiji, is a collapsed volcanic caldera.

For additional environment and climate trends, go to vitalsigns.worldwatch.org.

World Will Completely Miss 2010 Biodiversity Target

John Mulrow

Species classified by the International Union for Conservation of Nature (IUCN) as "threatened" increased by 2.1 percent in 2009, as 365 species were added to the organization's *Red List of Threatened Species*.[1] Only 2 species were removed from the list.[2] Since 1996, a total of 47,677 species of animals, plants, fungi, and protists (a group that includes protozoans and most algae) have been evaluated by the IUCN, and 17,291 of these are now considered threatened—a full 36 percent.[3] (See Table 1.)

All species evaluated by IUCN are given a threat rating based on a standardized set of data that includes population size and structure and geographic range.[4] Evaluated species for which data exist are divided into seven groups: least concern, near threatened, vulnerable, endangered, critically endangered, extinct in the wild, and extinct. Species in the three middle categories— vulnerable, endangered, and critically endangered—are collectively referred to as threatened. Species for which data are not available are not included in the seven groups, even if many of them are thought to be threatened.[5]

A complete evaluation of the world's 1.7 million known species—not to mention the 3–50 million species that have yet to be discovered—is extremely far off, but some species families

Table 1. Numbers of Threatened Species by Major Groups of Organisms, 1996–2009

Group	Species Described	Species Evaluated	Threatened Species	Threatened Species as Percentage of Evaluated
	(number)	(number)	(number)	(percent)
Vertebrates				
Mammals	5,490	5,490	1,142	21
Birds	9,998	9,998	1,223	12
Reptiles	9,084	1,677	469	28
Amphibians	6,433	6,285	1,895	30
Fishes	31,300	4,443	1,414	32
Invertebrates				
Insects	1,000,000	2,619	711	27
Corals	2,175	856	235	27
Horseshoe Crabs	4	4	0	0
Other invertebrates	303,071	4,136	1,693	41
Plants				
Gymnosperms	1,021	909	322	35
Flowering Plants	281,821	10,876	7,948	73
Other plants	38,370	366	230	63
Fungi and Protists				
All Fungi and Protists	51,563	18	9	50
TOTAL	1,740,330	47,677	17,291	36

Source: International Union for Conservation of Nature, The IUCN Red List of Threatened Species 2009.2, "Summary Statistics," Table 1.

have been completely described and evaluated, including birds, mammals, and amphibians.[6] Below the family level, reef-forming corals, conifers, cycads (palm-like plants), freshwater crabs, groupers, and most recently sturgeon have also been evaluated.[7] Currently, 30 percent of amphibians, 21 percent of mammals, and 12 percent of bird species are listed as threatened with extinction.[8] Of all groups evaluated, cycads and sturgeon have the highest proportion of threatened species, at 52 and 85 percent respectively.[9] (See Figure 1.)

Cycads are found in many tropical and subtropical areas. They are the oldest seed plants in the world.[10] The main threats they face are habitat disturbance, loss of habitat due to urbanization, and illegal removal by collectors.[11] In some cases, cycads become endangered due to the loss of pollinator insect species.[12]

Sturgeon are also an ancient species, among the oldest families of fish in the world.[13] Their unfertilized eggs (called roe) are highly prized in cuisine, most notably for caviar. The Beluga sturgeon of the Caspian Sea produce roe that can be worth up to $10,000 per kilogram for their use as black caviar.[14] Caviar demand has caused severe overexploitation of sturgeon populations throughout Europe and Asia.[15] As a result, 63 percent of sturgeon listed on the IUCN *Red List*

are considered "critically endangered."[16]

In 2009, some 42.5 percent of amphibian species were deemed to be "declining" in conservation status, while less than 1 percent were on the rise.[17] The leading threat to amphibians is habitat loss, affecting 61 percent of all species.[18] Logging or land clearing in tropical forests is behind much of this threat, as more than two thirds of all amphibians are tree-dwelling.[19] Pollution is a significant threat as well, due to amphibians' semi-aquatic lifestyle and their relatively low mobility.[20] In addition, the chytrid fungus—an invasive species unknown prior to 1998—has affected some amphibian populations and driven them to rapid population decline.[21] This fungus threatens around 8 percent of amphibian species.[22]

In the mammal category, 1,219 of the 5,488 species evaluated by IUCN are considered threatened, and 76 species are known to have become extinct since 1500.[23] Over 2,000 mammals are now facing dangerous rates of habitat loss, and a full 30 percent are declining in conservation status.[24] An extremely thorough evaluation process must be undertaken before a species can be deemed extinct. The little earth hutia, for example, a small rodent of Cuba that has not been observed in the wild for over 40 years, is considered critically endangered rather than extinct.[25]

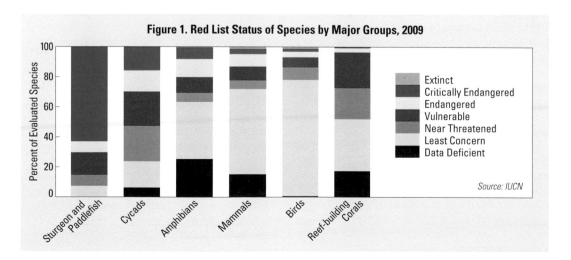

Figure 1. Red List Status of Species by Major Groups, 2009

Source: IUCN

Birds, while relatively less in danger than amphibians or cycads, are increasingly threatened overall.[26] Certain species, especially those that lay few eggs per clutch and have larger bodies, are extremely threatened.[27] Albatrosses and cranes are rated at 80 percent and 62 percent threatened, respectively.[28] Some 225 bird species have moved to a higher threat category at some point in the past 20 years, while only 32 are considered less threatened.[29]

Wetland birds of North America are among the few bird groups experiencing population gains.[30] The *Wetlands Birds Indicator* has risen steadily since 1970 thanks to wetland conservation and restoration as well as protections for certain hunted waterfowl.[31] Still, the wood stork of the Florida Everglades and other tropical and subtropical areas and the clapper rail, which favors estuaries, are two popular wetland species that remain federally listed as endangered.[32]

Birds of the Arctic, along with most other species in this region, are facing drastic changes to their habitats as climate change accelerates.[33] Arctic Sea ice has been declining since 1979, with the area of winter ice dropping an average of 8.9 percent per decade.[34] This represents a loss of habitat and an alteration of the chemical composition and temperature of the waters in which many species, such as the snowy owl and its prey, the lemming, survive.[35]

Reef-building corals also face potent threats from climate change. A significant portion of carbon dioxide (CO_2) emissions from human activities is taken up by the ocean, where the reaction between CO_2 and water increases the acidity of ocean water and disrupts the formation of corals' skeletons.[36] As CO_2 levels rise, corals' skeleton strength will weaken and reefs will be at greater risk of erosion. All known species of reef-building corals—numbering 845—were fully assessed for the first time in 2008.[37] Some 27 percent are listed as threatened and an additional 20 percent are near threatened, with deteriorating status.[38] Given the hundreds of thousands of plant and animal species that reside in reefs worldwide, the health of coral is yet another reason that CO_2 emissions must be stabilized.[39]

According to IUCN, the "species that are in greatest danger of climate-change driven extinction are those with high susceptibility to climatic changes, distribution ranges that will experience large climatic changes, and low adaptive capacity."[40] When evaluated for these traits, 35 percent of birds, 53 percent of amphibians, and 71 percent of reef-building corals were found to be facing severe threats to survival if climate change proceeds as predicted by the Intergovernmental Panel on Climate Change.[41]

Biodiversity was named in a 2009 study in *Nature* as the "planetary boundary" that humans have surpassed more than any other.[42] The study identified nine "Earth-system processes and associated thresholds which, if crossed, could generate unacceptable environmental change."[43] The proposed threshold for biodiversity loss was an extinction rate of 10 species per million per year, a boundary even higher than preindustrial extinction rates, which was estimated at a single species per million per year.[44] The study put the current extinction rate far above the boundary, at 100 species per million per year.[45] No other planetary boundary has been exceeded to such a great extent, although other boundaries with an impact on biodiversity have surpassed safe levels as well, including climate change and disruption of the nitrogen cycle.[46]

In 2010, the International Year of Biodiversity, the United Nations will evaluate progress on achieving a goal it set eight years ago: "to achieve by 2010 a significant reduction of the current rate of biodiversity loss at the global, regional and national level as a contribution to poverty alleviation and to the benefit of all life on Earth."[47] The status of that goal will be discussed at a meeting of the U.N. Convention on Biological Diversity in Japan in October, but it is already clear that the global biodiversity loss crisis is worsening. The number of threatened species is on track to rise again in 2010. In the first quarter of the year, IUCN had already added 25 species to the *Red List* and removed only 1.[48]

John Mulrow was a MAP Sustainable Energy Fellow at Worldwatch Institute in 2009-10.

Glacial Melt and Ocean Warming
Drive Sea Level Upward

John Mulrow and Alexander Ochs, with Shakuntala Makhijani

The average sea level around the world has risen a total of 222 millimeters (mm) since 1875, which means an annual rate of 1.7 mm.[1] (See Figure 1.) Yet at the end of this long period, from 1993 to 2009, the sea level rose 3.0 mm per year—a much faster rate.[2] An estimated 30 percent of the sea level increase since 1993 is a result of warmer ocean temperatures that cause the water to expand (thermal expansion).[3] Another 55 percent of the increase results from the melting of land-based ice, mainly from glaciers and the Greenland and Antarctic ice sheets.[4] (Sea ice that melts does not contribute to sea level rise, as the volume remains constant.)[5] The other 15 percent of the rise is due to changes in terrestrial freshwater dynamics, such as wetland drainage and lowered water tables.[6]

Ocean warming and land-based ice melt have happened in tandem with other climatic changes during the last century. These changes include rising atmospheric temperatures, acidification of ocean waters, and changes in seasonal water cycles—all of which are linked to a dramatic increase in atmospheric greenhouse gases. Prior to the industrial revolution, the atmospheric concentration of carbon dioxide—a major greenhouse gas—was steady at around 280 parts per million (ppm).[7] Since then, human activities such as the burning of fossil fuels and land use changes have boosted this concentration to over 385 ppm, nearly a 38-percent increase.[8]

The world's oceans absorb 80–90 percent of the excess solar radiation trapped on Earth by greenhouse gases.[9] But because the ocean's mass is so much greater than the atmosphere's, the oceans warm at a slower rate. From 1969 to 2009, atmospheric temperatures rose 0.36 degrees Celsius while the temperature in the upper ocean (the area down to 700 meters) rose 0.17 degrees.[10] (See Figure 2.)

From 1993 to 2003, thermal expansion of the ocean contributed approximately 1.6 mm per year to sea level rise, while land-based ice melt contributed 0.92 mm annually.[11] Then a marked reversal occurred from 2003 to 2008, when thermal expansion slowed to 0.34 mm per year and ice melt accelerated to 2.0 mm per year.[12] Most glaciated and ice-capped areas of the world are experiencing this rapid melt.

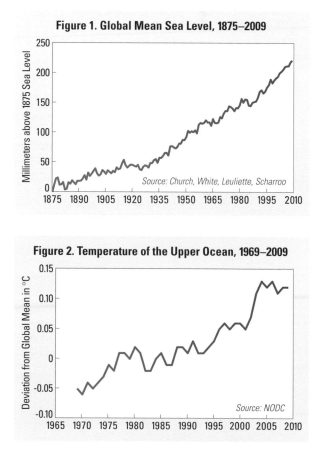

Figure 1. Global Mean Sea Level, 1875–2009

Source: Church, White, Leuliette, Scharroo

Figure 2. Temperature of the Upper Ocean, 1969–2009

Source: NODC

Glacial mass balance is typically expressed in meters of water equivalent—a measure of the loss or gain in average thickness from the previous year. The World Glacier Monitoring Service (WGMS) has long tracked the mass balance of 30 glaciers in nine different mountain ranges.[13] Over the past decade, their mass balance declined an average of 0.58 meters of water

equivalent per year, a rate more than twice that of the previous decade and four times that of the period 1976–85.[14] On average, the WGMS glaciers have lost 23 meters of water equivalent since 1980.[15] (See Figure 3.)

Glaciers in South America have shown significant losses, and in May 2009 the Chacaltaya Glacier in Bolivia melted away entirely.[16] The Chacaltaya was part of a glaciated mountain system in the Andes that has lost more than a third of its ice mass since 1983.[17] The world's largest tropical ice cap—the Quelccaya in southeastern Peru—is now smaller than it has been in more than 5,000 years.[18] Its largest outlet glacier, Qori Kalis, retreated approximately 60 meters per year from 1991 to 2005—a massive increase over its recorded retreat of 6 meters per year in the 1960s.[19]

Antarctica holds 86 percent of the world's land-based ice.[20] If the Antarctic ice sheet's entire volume of 24.7 million cubic kilometers were to melt and be converted to water, sea level could rise as much as 60 meters—although no one is predicting this is going to happen in the

Figure 3. Change in Average Glacier Mass for Monitored Glaciers, 1945–2008

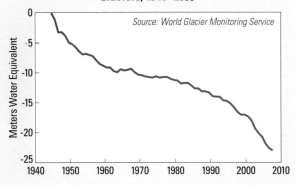

Source: World Glacier Monitoring Service

Table 1. Regions Threatened by Sea Level Rise

Threatened Region	Predicted Effects
Bangladesh	• 1 meter sea level rise could sink one fifth of the country's land mass and displace 20 million people • 28 centimeter sea level rise above 2000 levels would destroy 96 percent of tiger habitat in the Sundarban mangroves
Indonesia/Philippines	• Populations could be displaced—about 20 percent of the region lives in the low-elevation coastal zone • Heavily populated coastal regions, such as the city of Manila in the Philippines, could be threatened • Saltwater could affect freshwater resources and mangroves could be threatened
United States	• Sea level rise of 0.6 meters could eliminate 17–43 percent of U.S. wetlands and leave 3,540 kilometers of major roads and 1,450 kilometers of rail lines in the mid-Atlantic region at risk of regular inundation • Existing development in the coastal zone would experience increases in damages of 36–58 percent with a 0.3-meter sea level rise and 102–200 percent increase with a 0.9-meter rise • Rising sea levels will salinate aquifers along the Atlantic coast

Source: Compiled from various sources; see endnote 31.

near future.[21] From 1993 to 2008, the Antarctic ice sheet contributed to sea level rise at a rate of 0.55 mm per year, largely due to melting in Western Antarctica.[22] Eastern Antarctica is in fact gaining ice mass, though not fast enough to offset losses in the west.[23] This trend is believed to be a result of changing climate patterns in the Southern Hemisphere that affect the distribution of cold air and ocean water.[24]

The Fourth Assessment Report of the Intergovernmental Panel on Climate Change (IPCC), released in 2007, projected the sea level would rise between 0.18 and 0.59 meters during the twenty-first century.[25] This number did not incorporate projected changes in terrestrial freshwater dynamics, a source the IPCC has said could add another 0.17 meters of rise.[26] Several more-recent forecasts have shown that total sea level rise could be much more severe, reaching

1–2 meters over the course of the century.[27] Scientists have shown that rates of this magnitude are possible by analyzing geological evidence of sea level rise.[28] Similar rates of increase were seen during the last interglacial period (120,000 years ago), when the volume of terrestrial ice was roughly equal to today's.[29]

Worldwide, roughly 150 million people live in coastal areas within a meter of the sea, and 270 million live within 5 meters.[30] These are the people most immediately threatened with the rise of sea level, but the economic and environmental effects will extend to many others.[31] (See Table 1.) Roughly 10 percent of the world's population lives in coastal zones, and many of the most important economic hubs are coastal cities. In fact, 13 of the 20 megacities with populations greater than 10 million lie in coastal areas.[32]

Table 2. Regions Threatened by Glacial Melt

Threatened Region	Predicted Effects
Alps	• Alpine glacier cover will be nearly gone by 2050, changing irrigation and drinking water supply and crippling the European ski industry
Andes	• Andes tropical glaciers could disappear in 20 years if warming trends continue
	• Bolivia's glaciers could decrease 80 percent within a couple of decades
	• Serious consequences likely for water supplies to the region
	• Hydropower, which provides over half the electricity for Bolivia, Peru, and Ecuador, will be reduced
East African mountain ranges (Mts. Ruwenzori, Kenya, and Kilimanjaro)	• Kilimanjaro's glaciers will disappear within two decades if current conditions persist • Ice disappearance threatens dozens of plant and animal species in the Ruwenzori range, including leopards and chimpanzees
Himalayas	• Small glaciers could disappear by 2035 and many larger ones by the end of the century • There could be a shortage of Himalayan melt water that 700 million people rely on as main water source • Glacial lakes could experience outburst floods • Hydroelectricity production could decline
Rocky Mountains	• Some glaciers could disappear entirely • Diminished freshwater runoff and drinking water availability could affect key economic and densely populated regions, including already water-starved California • Changing water temperatures due to glacial shrinkage affect habitats of fish, insects, and other animals downstream

Source: Compiled from various sources; see endnote 36.

Varying temperature, ice melt, and ocean current trends create a disparity in sea level rise around the world. Southeast Asia, home to the densely populated Ganges-Brahmaputra and Mekong megadeltas as well as to many island nations, is one of the most vulnerable regions.[33] Sea level rise is happening there at a rate much faster than the global average. From 1992 to 2009 the South China Sea rose 4.6 mm per year and the Indonesian Seas rose 6.4 mm per year.[34] In contrast, the Bering Sea between Russia and Alaska has risen only 0.5 mm per year since 1993.[35]

The loss of glaciers will also threaten many parts of the world.[36] (See Table 2.) In the river basins of South Asia, 1.3 billion people depend on Himalayan glacier water as their main water source.[37] The temperature in the Himalayas has risen six times faster than the global average over the last century, threatening the long-term stability of the nearly 112,000 square kilometers of snow and ice that feed several major river systems.[38] In the Himalayas, as in other mountain regions of the world, pest increase, biodiversity loss, and forest fires are linked to changing water patterns.[39]

In the basins surrounding the Andes Mountains of South America, glaciers provide drinking water and irrigation supplies to 77 million people.[40] Glacial melt threatens the sustainability of these supplies and will also weaken the hydroelectricity potential of the rivers flowing out of the mountains. Researchers studying Andean glacier melt have noted the possibility of future civil unrest due to water scarcity in the region.[41]

John Mulrow was a MAP Sustainable Energy Fellow at Worldwatch Institute in 2009–10. Alexander Ochs is the Director of Worldwatch's Climate and Energy Program. Shakuntala Makhijani was an intern at the Institute.

Losses from Natural Disasters Decline in 2009

Petra Löw

In 2009, some 860 natural catastrophes occurred worldwide.[1] Given the 750 disasters registered in 2008, this represented an increase of 15 percent.[2] Last year had the fourth highest number of events in the period from 1980 to 2009.[3]

Some 92 percent of last year's events were weather-related disasters (compared with 82 percent in 2008): 42 percent were storms, 38 percent were floods, and 12 percent were other weather-related events, such as heat and cold waves, winter damage, droughts, and wildfires. The other 8 percent of total catastrophes in 2009 were geophysical events like earthquakes, volcanic eruptions, tsunamis, or subsidence.[4] This percentage distribution is in line with the long-term averages for these categories.[5] (See Figure 1.)

In 2009, overall economic losses from natural disasters totaled about $50 billion—the lowest since 2001—with insured losses at about $22 billion.[6] (See Figure 2.) Some 88 percent of the total losses and 98 percent of the insured ones were weather-related.[7] Only in the early 1980s and in the years 2000 and 2001 have overall losses been

this low, when adjusted for inflation.[8] The natural catastrophe figures for 2009 were marked by losses due to severe weather in areas with a high prevalence of insurance.[9]

The loss figures include a substantial number of weather-related natural catastrophes in Europe and the United States, with relatively high ratios of insured to economic losses in these regions.[10] Winter storm Klaus was the costliest event of the year, with total losses of $5.1 billion and insured losses of $3 billion.[11] About 40 percent of the overall losses and 60 percent of the insured ones occurred in the United States.[12] Especially severe storm events accounted for the high figures in North America, with eight of them each registering overall losses of $1 billion or more.[13]

Fatalities due to natural catastrophes amounted to 11,000 in 2009—one of the lowest figures since systematic recording began.[14] The long-term annual average of fatalities due to natural catastrophes since 1980 is around 57,000.[15] Some 82 percent of the fatalities last

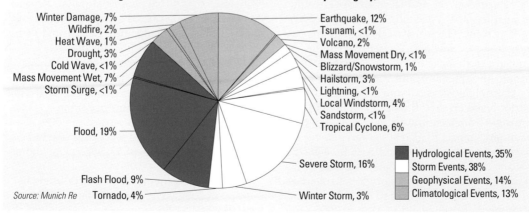

Figure 1. Distribution of Natural Disasters by Category, 1980–2009

Winter Damage, 7%
Wildfire, 2%
Heat Wave, 1%
Drought, 3%
Cold Wave, <1%
Mass Movement Wet, 7%
Storm Surge, <1%
Flood, 19%
Flash Flood, 9%
Source: Munich Re Tornado, 4%

Earthquake, 12%
Tsunami, <1%
Volcano, 2%
Mass Movement Dry, <1%
Blizzard/Snowstorm, 1%
Hailstorm, 3%
Lightning, <1%
Local Windstorm, 4%
Sandstorm, <1%
Tropical Cyclone, 6%
Severe Storm, 16%
Winter Storm, 3%

Hydrological Events, 35%
Storm Events, 38%
Geophysical Events, 14%
Climatological Events, 13%

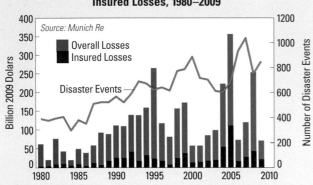

Figure 2. Natural Disaster Events and Economic and Insured Losses, 1980–2009

Figure 3. Distribution of Natural Disaster Events by Continent, 2009

year were caused by weather-related disasters.[16] By comparison, the average share of deaths due to weather-related disasters from 1980 to 2009 is 61 percent. The worst single event of the past year, however, was not weather-related: the Sumatra earthquake in Indonesia killed 1,200 people on September 30th.[17]

Natural disasters fall into six damage categories based on their financial and human impact—from a natural event with very little economic impact to a great natural disaster. Last year no event met the criteria for a great natural disaster, but 25 events were classified as devastating disasters (category 5), characterized by more than $500 million in overall losses or by more than 500 fatalities. Around 200 events

were classed as "medium severity" or "severe" catastrophes.[18]

The continental breakdown shows that Asia (290 events, for 34 percent) and North America including the Caribbean and Central America (250 events, for 30 percent) were the principal regions with natural catastrophes in 2009.[19] (See Figure 3.) Some 15 percent of events occurred in Europe (130 events); Africa and Australia each had 8 percent (70 events), while South America accounted for only 5 percent.[20]

The hurricane season in the Atlantic Ocean showed below-average activity, largely due to the onset of El Niño conditions in the tropical Pacific Ocean.[21] The long-term average from 1995 to 2009 is 14.3 tropical storms and 7.5 Atlantic hurricanes per season.[22] In 2009, nine named tropical storms developed in the Atlantic Ocean, three of which had hurricane force. Two of the hurricanes were major storms (Categories 3–5).[23] Hurricane Ida caused nominal losses to infrastructure in the United States and also affected El Salvador, Nicaragua, and Mexico. The overall loss from this single event was $1.5 billion.[24]

As with the weak hurricane season in the Atlantic Ocean, the situation in the northwest Pacific was 10–20 percent below the long-term climate norm. There were 25 tropical storms in this region, 14 typhoons, and 7 intense storms.[25] Typhoons Morakot, Ketsana, Melor, and Parma caused $7.5 billion in overall losses. China, the Philippines, Taiwan, and Viet Nam were the countries mainly affected.[26]

Thunderstorm losses in 2009 were the second highest on record, with 24 thunderstorm sequences causing about $14.6 billion in overall property damage.[27] In terms of wildfires, some 24,000 square kilometers burned in 2009, slightly more than in the preceding year but well below the average of 32,300 square kilometers a year for 2004–07.[28]

Some 91 percent of the natural disasters in Europe in 2009 were weather-related.[29] The overall loss—$12.5 billion—was mainly the result of four events. As noted earlier, winter storm Klaus caused $5.1 billion in losses in France, Spain, and Italy. In April, an earthquake in Italy destroyed the city of L´Aquila (overall loss of $2.5 billion). Parts of Western and Eastern Europe were hit by several severe storms and floods in June and July. And in Turkey, heavy rains caused a series of flash floods, with an overall loss of $550 million.[30]

In Africa, 96 percent of natural catastrophes were weather-related.[31] Floods in central and western Africa affected 1 million people in August and September and claimed more than 200 lives.[32]

The greater region of Australia and Oceania also was mainly affected by weather-related disasters in 2009 (over 90 percent).[33] Just as in 2008, Australia was mainly affected by extreme heat waves and major bush fires. More than 500 people died there because of natural disasters in 2009—the highest death toll in Australia for 100 years.[34] Especially damaging were the Victoria wildfires, also known as the "Black Saturday" fires, with more than 400 seats of fires and extreme dry conditions: 4,300 square kilometers of land burned, 3,400 houses were destroyed or damaged, 173 people were killed, and more than 7,500 people were displaced.[35]

The regional breakdown shows that the loss situation from natural and weather catastrophes in 2009 was well below the average of recent years and far from the extreme situations in 2004, 2005, and 2008.[36] But analysis by decade, comparing the 2000—09 period with the 1980s and 1990s, puts global disaster trends in a different light. (See Table 1.)

The percentage distribution of the number of events belonging to the main disaster groups (geophysical, meteorological, hydrological, and climatological events) shows that weather-related catastrophes—all of these events except for the geophysical ones—dominate the current decade, with 88 percent of the events. Storms (39 percent) and floods (37 percent) are followed by earthquakes (12 percent) and disasters like heat and cold waves, droughts, wildfires, and winter damages (12 percent).[37]

In terms of human losses, 63 percent (440,000 people) died in geophysical events (that is, events that were not weather-related).[38] Weather-related fatalities included 17 percent from storms, 8 percent from floods, and 12 percent from climatological events.[39] Asia registered the most fatalities in the last decade.[40]

During the past decade, 143 events caused at least $1 billion in overall losses, with losses from Hurricane Katrina reaching $125 billion (in current dollars).[41] Also, 5 of the 10 costliest disasters between 1980 and 2009 occurred in the last 10 years.[42] North America—especially the United States—Asia, and Europe mainly felt the financial impact of natural disasters.[43] Weather-

Table 1. Natural and Weather-related Disasters in 1980s, 1990s, and 2000s

Disasters	1980–89	1990–99	2000–09
All Natural Disasters			
Number	4,140 disasters	6,500 disasters	7,800 disasters
Overall losses*	$483 billion	$1.2 trillion	$1.1 trillion
Fatalities	456,000 deaths	450,000 deaths	700,000 deaths
Weather-related Disasters			
Number	3,500 disasters	5,500 disasters	6,900 disasters
Overall losses*	$366 billion	$900 billion	$870 billion
Fatalities	370,000 deaths	340,000 deaths	260,000 deaths

*Losses in 2009 dollars.
Source: Munich Re, GeoRisksResearch, February 2010.

Table 2. Costliest Hurricanes in the Atlantic Ocean, 2000–2009

Dates	Event	Affected Area	Overall Losses	Insured Losses	Deaths
			(million dollars, in current dollars)		
25–30 August 2005	Katrina, and storm surge	United States	125,000	62,000	1,322
6–14 September 2008	Ike	United States, Cuba, Haiti, Dominican Republic, Turks and Caicos, Bahamas	38,000	18,500	168
7–21 September 2004	Ivan	Barbados, Cayman Islands, Cuba, Dominican Republic, Grenada, Haiti, Jamaica, St. Lucia, St. Vincent and the Grenadines, Trinidad and Tobago, Venezuela, Colombia, United States, Mexico	23,000	13,800	125
19–24 October 2005	Wilma	Bahamas, Cuba, Haiti, Jamaica, Mexico, United States	22,000	12,500	42
11–14 August 2004	Charley	United States (esp. Florida), Cuba, Jamaica, Cayman Islands	18,000	8,000	36
20–24 September 2005	Rita, and storm surge	United States	16,000	12,100	10
1–9 September 2004	Frances	United States, Bahamas, Canada, Turks and Caicos, Cayman Islands, Canada	12,000	5,500	39
21 Aug. – 3 Sept. 2008	Gustav	Cuba, Dominican Republic, Haiti, Jamaica, United States	10,000	3,500	139

Source: Munich Re.

related disasters—at $870 billion—were the largest contributors to the total amount of $1.1 trillion (in 2010 values), with storms accounting for 57 percent, floods 17 percent, and climatological events 8 percent.[44] Most of the costliest events were hurricanes in the Atlantic Ocean, including Katrina (2005), Ike (2008), Ivan (2004), Wilma (2005), Charley (2004), and Rita (2005). (See Table 2.)

In comparison with the 1980s, the last decade had twice as many total events and weather-related disasters.[45] Inflation-adjusted overall losses have doubled too, whereas the highest increase occurred between the 1980s and the 1990s.[46] According to the United Nations International Strategy for Disaster Reduction, the last decade was the deadliest—by a factor of 1.5—mostly driven by geophysical events.[47]

Petra Löw is a Geographer and NatCat analyst at the Munich Reinsurance Company.

Bottled Water Consumption Growth Slows

Alice McKeown Jaspersen

Nearly 200 billion liters of bottled water were consumed worldwide in 2008.[1] (See Figure 1.) Although the figure was up more than 5 percent over 2007, it marks a decline in the growth rate over previous years, which saw annual gains of 6–10 percent.[2] The rise in per capita consumption also tapered off to a rate near 4 percent, reaching 30 liters per person.[3] Most of the bottles sold contain non-sparkling water, which accounts for 90 percent of the total volume.[4]

The United States continues to lead the world in bottled water use, accounting for more than 16 percent of the global total.[5] (See Figure 2.) However, consumption there contracted by 1 percent to reach 32.8 billion liters, the only decline in the last 10 years.[6] Producers' revenues also dropped, down 3.2 percent to $11.2 billion.[7] Overall, though, their revenues have increased 83 percent since 2000.[8]

Elsewhere in the Americas, Mexico is now the second largest market in the world, with 24.6 billion liters or 12 percent of the global total in 2008.[9] And Brazil is the fourth largest, at 14.2 billion liters and 7 percent of the global total.[10]

Europe includes 4 of the top 10 largest national markets: Italy, Germany, France, and Spain.[11] But unlike other countries that have experienced significant growth in the last few years, countries in Europe tend to have slow or negative growth rates due in part to a longer history of bottled water usage.[12] For example, consumption in Germany grew 4 percent in 2008 following a contraction of 2 percent the year before.[13]

Asia accounts for 26 percent of global water use.[14] (See Figure 3.) China has experienced the strongest average growth over the past five years of all the top-10 market countries.[15] It is now the third largest global market, with annual consumption of 19.7 billion liters.[16] Indonesia had the largest single-year growth of the top 10: more than a 20 percent increase.[17]

Over the last decade, the top 10 countries have consistently accounted for 74 percent of global consumption of bottled water.[18]

Mexico may be second in the world in total consumption, but it became number one in consumption per capita, with an average of nearly

Figure 1. Global Bottled Water Consumption, 1999–2008

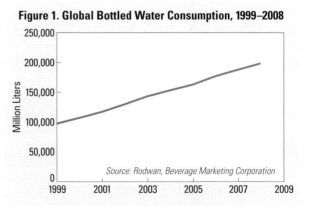

Source: Rodwan, Beverage Marketing Corporation

Figure 2. Global Bottled Water Consumption, Leading Countries, 1999–2008

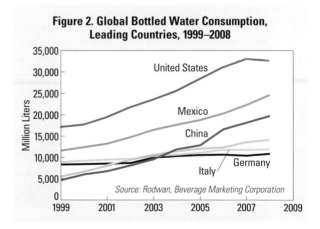

Source: Rodwan, Beverage Marketing Corporation

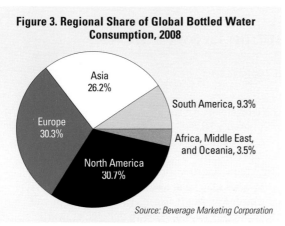

Figure 3. Regional Share of Global Bottled Water Consumption, 2008

Asia 26.2%

South America, 9.3%

Europe 30.3%

Africa, Middle East, and Oceania, 3.5%

North America 30.7%

Source: Beverage Marketing Corporation

224 liters per person.[19] (See Figure 4.) Italy is second, followed by the United Arab Emirates, although that country saw a significant decline in 2008.[20] Per capita consumption declined by nearly 2 percent in the United States to reach 108 liters.[21]

Although many regions still have significant diversity in bottled water supplies, the trend is toward greater consolidation, with four companies controlling a large stake of the global market.[22] In 2008, Nestlé Waters had the second largest sales in the global drinks market at $26.5 billion.[23] Soft drink giants Coca-Cola and PepsiCo are also likely to further expand their bottled water marketing in the international arena, following their success in the U.S. market.[24]

The bottled water industry attributes rising consumption to factors such as health, safety, and convenience, even though these perceived benefits may also be available through tap water. In the United States, growing use of bottled water has been accompanied by reduced demand for carbonated soft drinks over the last decade.[25] This may indicate that consumers are still looking for beverages on the go and are shifting to water as a healthy alternative. A poll conducted in the United States in 2002 indicated that the taste of water was also a growing factor in choosing bottled water.[26] In developing countries, in contrast, bottled water may provide a source of safe drinking water not

otherwise easily accessible.[27]

Industry experts point to the difficult economy and environmental concerns as two factors in slowed bottled water growth, especially in the United States.[28]

Most bottled water is sold in plastic containers, with polyethylene terephthalate (PET) packaging the clear leader.[29] In the United States, single-serve PET water makes up 60 percent of total bottled water volume, while all types of plastic account for some 96.6 percent of water packaging.[30] By contrast, in Germany most bottled water is sold in returnable glass bottles, due in part to rules requiring a high deposit on cans and nonreturnable bottles.[31] Total PET bottle recycling collection is now around 40 percent in Europe and 27 percent in the United States.[32]

Some companies are developing plant-based plastics for beverage containers, including bottled water. Plant-based plastics, which can be made partially or entirely from biological materials, currently make up less than 1 percent of total global plastics use, but they are expected to grow in popularity as the price of oil rebounds and as the materials become more widely available.[33] In 2009 Coca-Cola unveiled its PlantBottle, made partially from sugar cane, and the company aims to produce 2 billion of the containers by the end of 2010.[34] Other efforts to reduce plastic reliance include "lightweighting"—reducing the amount of plastics used in any given bottle.[35]

Producing bottled water requires significant energy inputs, amounting to as much as 2,000 times that required to produce tap water, in the case of the United States.[36] If locally bottled water is consumed in 1-liter PET bottles, the production of the bottles accounts for 71 percent of the total energy used.[37] If bottled water is shipped over long distances before being consumed, the energy requirements for transporting it can outpace those for bottle manufacture, in some cases doubling the overall energy use.[38] One study estimates that annual bottled water consumption in the United States requires energy inputs equal to between 32 million and

54 million barrels of oil.[39] At the global level, these inputs are tripled.[40]

Bottled water can also harbor impurities and contaminants. A 2008 study revealed disinfection byproducts, medications, fertilizer residue, and other chemicals in bottled water sold in the United States.[41] Other studies have raised concerns over residues from plastics that may be found in the bottles, including DEHP, a phthalate known to increase risk of cancer, and bisphenol A, an endocrine disruptor, which may leach from some large water jugs.[42]

Campaigns against bottled water usage have led some consumers to turn back to tap water.[43] Some high-end restaurants in San Francisco and New York have stopped carrying bottled water, opting instead for filtration systems that are seen as more eco-friendly.[44] Some municipalities have joined this movement, banning their own purchases of bottled water in places like Seattle and San Francisco.[45] And in 2009 Bundanoon,

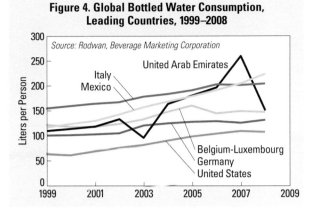

Figure 4. Global Bottled Water Consumption, Leading Countries, 1999–2008

in Australia, voted to forbid bottled water sales entirely in its community.[46]

Alice McKeown Jaspersen was the Director of Vital Signs Online.

Food and Agriculture Trends

NASA/GSFC/METI/ERSDAC/JAROS, and US/Japan ASTER Science Team

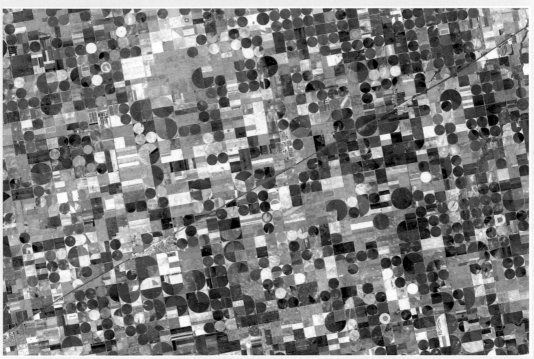

Center-pivot irrigation circles in Kansas.

For additional food and agricultural trends, go to vitalsigns.worldwatch.org.

Grain Production Strong But Fails to Set Record

Alice McKeown Jaspersen

In 2009, farmers produced a near-record crop of grains worldwide: more than 2.25 billion tons.[1] (See Figure 1.) While this was a decline from the all-time high set in 2008, the grain crop has had a 21-percent increase since 2000 and a 180-percent increase since recordkeeping began in 1961.[2] Most of the gains made over time are due to increased yields, as the total amount of land dedicated to annual grain harvests has remained relatively stable.[3]

Grains include large crops of wheat, rice, and maize—all in the top 10 list by value of annual production—and are used for human food, animal feed, and industrial products.[4] Global per capita production declined slightly in 2009 to reach 330 kilograms grown per person.[5] However, grains consumed by people for food increased slightly over the previous year to reach 152.1 kilograms per person.[6]

Asia stayed the global leader in grain production, growing nearly 44 percent of the world's crop in 2009.[7] (See Table 1.) Rice continues to be the biggest crop in the region and accounted for 42 percent of all grains grown there.[8]

The Americas and Europe grew 28 and 21 percent respectively of the global grain crop in 2009.[9] The largest crop in the Americas is coarse grains, a category that includes maize, barley, sorghum, rye, oats, and others.[10] Here the single largest crop was maize, which accounted for more than 70 percent of grain production.[11] In Europe, the main crop is also in coarse grains, but with a greater emphasis on barley instead of maize.[12]

Africa grew only 6 percent of the global grain crop, with a focus on coarse grains like sorghum.[13] Oceania was the smallest regional grain producer, with nearly 2 percent of the global crop, dominated by wheat production.[14]

Developing countries grew over 54 percent of the global grain crop in 2009, in line with the average of the previous three years.[15] These countries dominated rice production, growing 96 percent of the global crop.[16] Within this group, the least developed countries have been steadily increasing their share of grain production, with 141.4 million tons in 2009—up 3.6 percent over 2008.[17]

The way grain crops are used remained stable over the past year, with about 47 percent going to human consumption and 35 percent used to feed industrial livestock.[18] Feed use is expected to remain level in the near term because of a combination of a slight decline in industrial countries due to the economic recession and a growth in developing countries because of increasing meat consumption.[19] Demand for grain-based biofuels such as ethanol is expected to grow and remain strong due to government mandates to move in that direction and other policy incentives around the world.[20]

Maize is the largest grain crop and

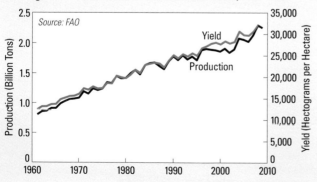

Figure 1. World Grain Production and Yield, 1961–2009

Source: FAO

accounted for 36 percent of global grain production (815.1 million tons).[21] The largest use of maize is for livestock feed, although it is also used for food and industrial products and more recently as a feedstock for biofuels.[22] The United States was the largest single producer, growing more than 40 percent of the global maize crop in 2009.[23] (See Figure 2.) The United States also dominates the maize trade, with on average 60 percent of total global maize exports over the last several years.[24] With this large market, maize accounts for approximately 11 percent by value of all U.S. agricultural exports each year.[25]

Grain prices have declined significantly from the record highs reached in 2008.[26] (See Figure 3.) But prices at the end of 2009 were still 19 percent higher than three years earlier, and 66 percent higher than at the end of 2004.[27] Although cereal and grain prices tend to rise and fall in line with the general food price index, grain prices are typically more volatile. In one recent example, grain prices fell in early 2010 because of crop prospects and strong supplies and were down 9 percent over December 2009.[28] But summer scares over drought and export bans in Russia sent the price of wheat futures up dramatically.[29] Recent projections show that wheat and coarse grain prices over the next 10 years will be 15–40 percent higher than the average seen in the period 1997–2006.[30]

World grain stocks continued their recovery in 2009, up nearly 6 percent over the previous year.[31] (See Figure 4.) The related stocks-to-use ratio that compares global stocks to annual consumption remained steady at around 23 percent, a positive sign for global food security and global grain stability.[32] Global trade in grains—based on export data—fell by nearly 7 percent in 2009.[33]

Grains supply approximately 70 percent of human calories, making them an essential component of global food security.[34] When coupled with the growing problem of global hunger—there are now more than 1 billion hungry people worldwide—finding ways to improve grain production and distribution becomes funda-

Table 1. Grain Production by Region, 2000–2009

Region	2000	2006	2007	2008	2009	Growth over 2000
	(million tons)					(percent)
Asia	814.7	926.6	954.1	980.7	980.6	20
Africa	105.8	141.4	130.3	143.7	150.4	42
Americas	521.5	533.6	632.6	634.8	623.1	19
Europe	383.8	402.3	390.1	503.2	463.5	21
Oceania	35.0	19.9	22.9	34.6	35.5	1
World	1,860.8	2,023.8	2,130.1	2,297.0	2,253.1	21

Source: "Production-Crops," in U.N. Food and Agriculture Organization (FAO), FAOSTAT Statistical Database, at faostat.fao.org, updated 16 December 2009; FAO, Food Outlook, June 2010, p. 62.

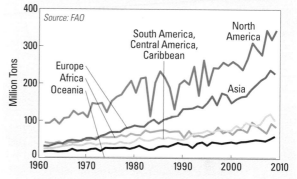

Figure 2. Maize Production by Region, 1961–2009

mental to addressing food security and widespread undernourishment.[35] The Food and Agriculture Organization (FAO) estimates that post-harvest losses of food crops range from 15 to 50 percent and has begun working with local communities on several innovative solutions to reduce food waste.[36] In Afghanistan, for example, FAO provided metallic silos to local families for grain storage that reduced post-harvest losses from 15–20 percent down to 1–2 percent.[37] Simple storage improvements made by communities that protect harvests from pests and moisture without large investments can also be effective, as seen in storage bags used by farmers in Niger to protect the legume cowpeas.[38]

Figure 3. World Food and Cereals Price Index, 1990–2010

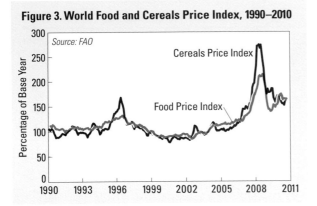

Figure 4. World Grain Stocks, 1960–2009

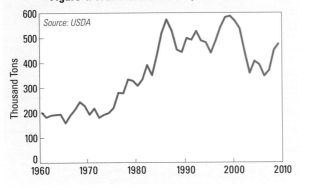

availability are the development of heat-tolerant varieties and the spread of conservation practices that reduce tilling, increase crop residue retention, and use crop rotations, among others.[40] Success with conservation innovations has already been seen for wheat and rice farmers in South Asia, but more efforts are needed for further research and outreach to farmers.[41]

Another area of research that might help address climate change and provide additional environmental benefits is the development of perennial versions of annual grain crops such as wheat, rice, maize, and sorghum. Perennial crops could potentially overcome many of the disadvantages of annual grain production by increasing soil carbon and the absorption of precipitation, requiring fewer chemical inputs, extending the growing season, and reducing erosion.[42] However, these types of plants are not expected to be available for 20 years—and only if significant research scales up.[43]

Creation of a global food reserve system also may be able to address problems of grain production and distribution. Although reserve systems have been tried—and abandoned—in the past, there is a growing resurgence of interest.[44] These reserves would supply food aid during humanitarian disasters and emergencies, and would also be able to reduce price volatility by selling and buying grain to change the market.[45] Current discussions include national, regional, and international roles, physical versus cash stocks, and management and implementation.[46]

Alice McKeown Jaspersen was the director of Vital Signs Online.

Climate change is likely to affect grain production as temperatures rise, extreme weather events like floods and droughts increase, and the distribution of available water and precipitation patterns shift.[39] Two agricultural innovations that may help prevent a reduction in grain

Meat Production and Consumption
Continue to Grow

Alexandra Tung

Global meat production increased by only 0.8 percent in 2009 to 281.5 million tons, a slow-down from the 2.4 percent growth rate of 2008.[1] But the increase continued the steady growth of the past decade. Since 2000, global meat production has risen by 20 percent.[2] (See Figure 1.)

The production of beef increased by less than a tenth of 1 percent in 2009, reaching 65.1 million tons.[3] The United States remains the largest beef producer, but output there is expected to fall by 1 percent in 2010, below 12 million tons, due to rising feed costs.[4]

Total production of pork—the largest category of meat (see Figure 2)—remained steady in 2009 at 106.1 million tons.[5] Half of the world's pork comes from China.[6] Production in Vietnam and the Philippines is on the rise, while pork production in the United States is expected to decline in 2010 by 3 percent.[7]

Global production of poultry was 91.3 million tons in 2009, and is expected to reach 94.8 million tons in 2010, an increase of 2.7 percent.[8] The United States remains the largest producer of poultry and eggs.[9] Output in China, India, Thailand, and Brazil is expected to grow by around 4 percent in 2010.[10] In the last category of meat, some 13 million tons of sheep and other miscellaneous meat products were produced in 2009.[11]

The Food and Agriculture Organization (FAO) and the Organisation for Economic Co-operation and Development project that meat production will continue to expand at 1.9 percent annually for the next 10 years.[12] Some 89 percent of production growth is expected to occur in developing countries, including China, Brazil, and sub-Saharan Africa, because intensive industrial production systems in industrial countries and new food safety and animal health regulations pose barriers for growth there.[13]

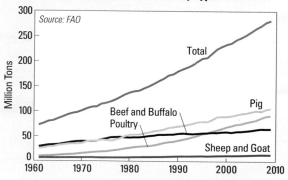

Figure 1. World Meat Production, by Type, 1961–2009

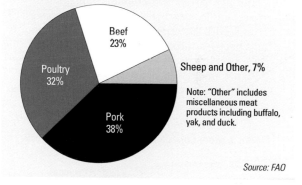

Figure 2. World Meat Production by Source, 2009

With varied growth in production volume in different geographic regions, world meat trade is expected to rise. Australia and Brazil were the largest net exporters of beef in 2009.[14] Denmark is the world's second largest producer of pork and is expected to increase its exports to China, following a recent trade agreement.[15] By 2019, world meat exports are projected to be 22 percent higher than in 2007–09.[16]

Growth in consumption is expected to continue as well. On average, people around the world eat 41.6 kilograms of meat and meat products a year.[17] At the projected annual growth rate of 2.4 percent through 2019, livestock product consumption will grow faster than that of other major agricultural products (and, interestingly, faster than projected production, some 1.9 percent annually).[18] Most of the growth will take place in developing countries, where 60 percent of meat is consumed.[19] But per person consumption in those countries, at 31.3 kilograms per year, is less than half of the 80.1 kilograms per person in industrial countries.[20] (See Figure 3.)

Worldwide pork consumption is currently at 28 kilograms per person a year; it is likely to grow 1.8 percent annually through 2019.[21] Most of the increase will occur in developing countries in Asia due to the growth of cities and higher incomes.[22]

Globally, people eat on average 11 kilograms of poultry a year, and consumption is expected to increase at an annual rate of 2.4 percent through 2019.[23] Developing countries will account for nearly 83 percent of this increase.[24] In industrial countries, consumption of poultry is likely to surpass that of pork.[25]

Beef has the lowest per capita consumption figure among the major meat commodities: 9 kilograms a year on average worldwide.[26] There are some exceptions to this in East Africa and Asia, where beef is a traditionally important commodity. As with overall meat consumption trends, continued growth is projected to occur mainly in developing countries, at an average of 2 percent through 2019.[27]

Livestock production holds great importance globally for improving livelihoods and ensuring food security. It employs 1.3 billion people worldwide and contributes 40 percent of gross global agricultural product.[28] Livestock production is responsible for one third of global protein intake.[29] Smallholder livestock keepers account for almost 20 percent of the world's population, and according to FAO, up to 82 percent of the rural poor in Asia, Africa, and Latin America keep livestock.[30] At 4.8 million tons per year, livestock production is essential for ensuring the livelihoods of a large percentage of the African population.[31]

While smallholder livestock production in developing countries primarily uses extensive grazing areas, industrial countries tend to promote confined animal production systems that emphasize high input and output.[32] Livestock production uses 30 percent of the Earth's ice-free land surface, compared with only 8 percent used for crops grown for human consumption.[33] A third of arable land is used to produce feed for livestock, and in sub-Saharan Africa, increasing foreign investment and large-scale land acquisitions are expected to mean a growth in livestock feed production.[34]

Livestock production requires heavy usage of water resources, accounting for 31 percent of total water use in agriculture.[35] Water use for feed crop production in developing countries alone can range from 1 trillion to 2 trillion cubic meters per year, while cattle, sheep, and goat production requires 536 billion cubic meters a year.[36]

Total greenhouse gas emissions from livestock and feed production are several times higher in industrial countries than in developing ones. This is due to the extensive use of carbon-based fuels and to land use changes, such as livestock-linked deforestation in Latin America.[37]

Figure 3. Meat Consumption per Person, 1961–2009

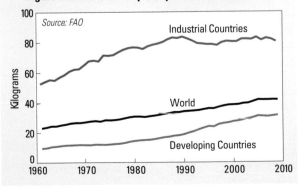

Industrial farming practices, coupled with climate change and growing human and animal populations, can also increase the incidence of animal and human disease. Global warming, in particular, is providing new and more suitable environments for the spread of infectious diseases.[38] Diseases that have crossed from domestic animals to humans include the avian influenza (H5N1), swine flu (H1N1), foot-and-mouth disease, mad cow disease (bovine spongiform encephalopathy), and Rift Valley fever (RVF).

The highest human fatality rate from avian influenza is found in Indonesia, but new cases have been found in 2010 in Egypt, China, Vietnam, and Cambodia.[39] To date, there have been 507 confirmed cases and 302 deaths worldwide.[40] More than 214 countries, overseas territories, and communities have reported confirmed cases of swine flu, which originated from pigs in Asia.[41] Over 18,449 deaths have been reported.[42] This H1N1 flu accounts for 27 percent of flu cases in Ghana.[43]

Foot-and-mouth disease also continues to thrive. In China, 16 provinces experienced outbreaks in 2010.[44] A recent outbreak in Botswana, which infected hundreds of cattle, was fortunately contained through vaccination programs.[45] Luckily, there have been few new cases of mad cow disease in 2010. The United Kingdom had just seven cases, while France reported four new infections.[46] To date, there have been 170 human cases of variant Creutzfeldt-Jakob disease acquired from contact with or consumption of infected cattle in the United Kingdom.[47]

Rift Valley fever is another virus that can be spread from animals to humans through mosquitoes or contact with the blood or organs of infected animals.[48] Globally, it has resulted in a total of 14,128 cases in animals and 8,721 deaths to date.[49] RVF continues to affect cattle, goats, and sheep most severely in South Africa, where 13,902 cases and 8,581 deaths have been recorded and significant economic losses have been incurred.[50]

Human health is also affected by the use of antibiotics in industrial farming operations, as this is linked to antibiotic resistance in humans.[51]

Food crops such as potatoes and corn are particularly susceptible to antibiotics contamination from soils spread with manure that contains antibiotics.[52] A 2009 study in U.S. swine farms found that 70 percent of swine sampled carry methicillin-resistant S. aureus (MRSA) bacteria, and 64 percent of workers from the same farm systems tested positive for MRSA.[53] Annually, some 100,000 people die from hospital-acquired infections that stem from the overuse of antibiotics, with MRSA being one of the main culprits.[54] Strains of drug-resistant E. coli in patients are found to be virtually identical to those in beef and poultry, suggesting that humans can be affected through meat consumption as well as through contact.[55] In 2006, the European Union started phasing out the use of antibiotics for purposes other than treating diseases, and in 2010 the U.S. Food and Drug Administration issued draft guidance for the use of antimicrobials in the food industry.[56]

Recent studies reiterate long-standing evidence that points toward long-term health consequences of diets high in meats. Processed meat was found to cause a higher incidence of chronic diseases related to overweight and obesity, such as coronary heart disease and diabetes, than fresh meats did.[57] Another study suggested that improved weight management might be achieved through decreasing meat consumption.[58]

The potential links between high meat consumption and human health problems have prompted efforts to follow a more plant-centered diet. The city of Ghent in Belgium, for example, started promoting "Meatless Thursdays" with 90,000 street maps to vegetarian restaurants in 2009.[59] And 2009 marked the second year that 80,000 children in Baltimore schools were served meat-free meals on Mondays.[60] In April 2010, the San Francisco Board of supervisors signed a resolution supporting meatless Mondays.[61] Thirty-two U.S. hospitals have signed on to the Balanced Menu Challenge, which requires a commitment to reduce meat purchases by 20 percent.[62]

Reducing the ecological consequences of

meat production requires a change in current production systems. Selective breeding for animals that yield higher quantities of meat and milk has led to the extinction of more than 60 breeds of cattle, goats, pigs, horses, and poultry in the first few years of the twenty-first century.[63] UNESCO estimates that 21 percent of the world's 7,000 livestock breeds are at risk of extinction.[64] Many species under threat, such as the Lulu cattle from Nepal and the Criolla Mora sheep from Colombia, possess characteristics valuable for climate change adaption, such as resistance to disease and the ability to thrive in drought conditions in hotter temperatures.[65]

For more sustainable meat production, deci-sionmakers could consider measures to help farmers adopt alternatives that maintain productivity while conserving water and preventing water contamination. Some examples of these alternatives include selecting indigenous breeds, preserving natural grasslands, and adopting eco-agricultural approaches such as agricultural systems that incorporate livestock and vegetation.[66] Opting for these practices could reduce the impact of livestock production on the environment and help protect biodiversity.[67]

Alexandra Tung was an intern at Worldwatch Institute.

Global Fish Production Continues to Rise

Stephanie Pappas

Total global fish production, including wild capture and aquaculture, rose to approximately 159 million tons in 2008, the most recent year with data.[1] This is a 1.27 percent increase from 2007 production levels.[2] (See Figure 1.) Aquaculture, after growing steadily for the last four decades, now contributes nearly half of the fish produced worldwide and is expected to catch up to wild capture by 2012.[3] Overall, 77 percent of fish production is for human consumption; the remainder is used for non-food production, mostly in the fishmeal and fish oil industries and for livestock feed.[4]

In 2006, the average global per capita fish production was 3.3 tons per year.[5] Some regions, however, had per capita production rates well above that. Europe and Oceania reported per capita output at 21.4 and 25.1 tons per year respectively.[6] While the Asia region only produced 2.5 tons per year per person, it does contain 85.8 percent of the world's fishers and fish farmers.[7] In stark contrast, Europe and Oceania only have 1.7 and 0.1 percent of the world's fishers and fish farmers.[8]

Global per capita fish consumption has been increasing steadily from an average of 9.9 kilograms in the 1960s to an average of 14.4 kilograms in the 1990s and 17.1 kilograms in 2009.[9] Fish provided about 7.6 percent of the animal protein consumed by humans in North and Central America, more than 11 percent in Europe, 19 percent in Africa, and 21 percent in Asia.[10] Rising incomes, improved infrastructure, and diversification in diets are pushing developing countries toward significantly higher fish product consumption.[11] In many small island developing nations and coastal countries, such as Bangladesh, Cambodia, and Ghana, fish supply at least 50 percent of the total animal protein intake.[12] Fish and fishmeal also provide a

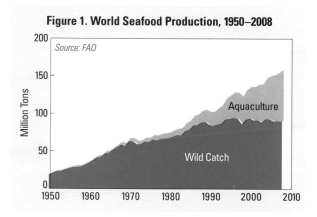

Figure 1. World Seafood Production, 1950–2008

crucial and cheap source of animal protein and micronutrients for HIV/AIDS patients in developing countries.[13]

The proportions of overexploited, depleted, and recovering fishery stocks have remained relatively constant for the last 10–15 years.[14] In 2007, some 28 percent of the world's marine fish stocks were categorized as overexploited, depleted, or recovering from depletion.[15] As a result, these fish were yielding less than their maximum potential. Another 52 percent of marine fish stocks were fully exploited and yielding catches that were at or close to their maximum sustainable limits.[16] Thus only about 20 percent of stocks were considered to be moderately exploited or underexploited with the possibility of producing more.[17]

Most of the stocks for the top 10 species—including the Alaska pollack and the yellowfin tuna, which account for approximately 30 percent of the global marine capture production in terms of quantity—are categorized as exploited or overexploited.[18] (See Figure 2.) In response to decreasing population numbers, the Convention on International Trade in Endangered

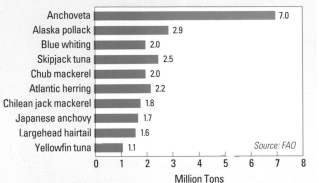

Figure 2. Top 10 Species from Marine Capture Production, 2006

Species	Million Tons
Anchoveta	7.0
Alaska pollack	2.9
Blue whiting	2.0
Skipjack tuna	2.5
Chub mackerel	2.0
Atlantic herring	2.2
Chilean jack mackerel	1.8
Japanese anchovy	1.7
Largehead hairtail	1.6
Yellowfin tuna	1.1

Source: FAO

Species of Wild Fauna and Flora has proposed banning global trade of the most at-risk species, including the Atlantic bluefin tuna, a top value-producing fish.[19]

With nearly 64 percent of the open ocean beyond national jurisdictions, high seas marine protected areas (HSMPAs) need to be created and promoted to help prevent overexploitation of fish stocks.[20] High seas are open-access common zones, beyond the reach of individual countries' economic exclusion zones. They are only regulated via international or regional agreements and often fall victim to overfishing, oil and gas exploration, seabed mining, and pollution.[21] HSMPAs safeguard breeding grounds and create migration corridors that allow fish stock the chance to recharge and that help maintain optimal population sizes.[22]

Inland fisheries continue to increase production.[23] In 2006, inland fisheries contributed 11 percent of the global capture production, and landings from inland waters remain essential parts of the diets of both rural and urban people, especially in developing countries.[24] Also, benefits from inland fisheries tend to remain with local communities, making their socio-economic value disproportionately higher than other fisheries.[25]

Careful maintenance will help guarantee that inland fisheries are responsibly developed and continue to be adequate sources of food.[26] For example, land use practice changes around Lake Victoria in Africa have increased the input of nutrients in the water and the level of primary production.[27] Currently, the increased food supply has helped maintain fish production levels, but if nutrient levels continue to rise, the loss of habitat and oxygen will place the entire lake ecosystem in jeopardy.[28] In Southeast Asia, the Mekong River basin continues to sustain the largest inland fishery in the world; however, the increased number of fishers, habitat fragmentation, and dam building threaten the integrity of the ecosystem.[29]

While capture fishery production growth stagnated in the 1980s, aquaculture has maintained an approximate annual growth rate of 8.7 percent since 1970.[30] Aquaculture is growing faster than any other animal food-producing sector, and it is set to surpass beef production by 2010.[31] Aquaculture's growth, however, is not uniform across the globe. (See Figure 3.) Aquaculture is growing approximately six times faster in developing countries than in industrial ones.[32]

Salmon and shrimp continue to dominate aquaculture production. Almost two thirds of the world's salmon is produced this way, with Norway and Chile contributing the most.[33] One third of the shrimp consumed globally is from aquaculture, and that percentage grows every year.[34] At 73 percent, tilapia has one of the highest aquaculture production rates, and it also has one of the fastest-growing demand rates of any fish product.[35]

Fisheries and aquaculture play a vital role in the livelihoods of millions of people. Over the last three decades, growth in employment in primary fisheries and aquaculture has exceeded that in the traditional agriculture sector.[36] An estimated 43.5 million people are permanently employed in the primary production of fish and another 4 million have jobs seasonally as fishers and fish processors.[37] Including people working in secondary production—fish processing, marketing, and related service industries—the total employment estimate is 170 million.[38]

Women in particular benefit from the employment opportunities and the household food security that fisheries and aquaculture can provide. Over half of all full- and part-time fishers and fish farmers are women.[39] Most often they are employed in secondary production and fishery-related service sectors, such as making and mending nets, baskets, and pots and baiting hooks.[40] Women are unlikely to work in commercial offshore or deep-sea waters; however, they are more involved with coastal and inland fishing activities.[41]

As demand for fish products continues to rise, public concerns about aquaculture practices and wild fish stock viability are growing. The Chilean government recently revealed that in 2007 and 2008 it used over 300,000 kilograms of antibiotics a year in its farmed salmon industry—600 times more than was used in Norway, the leading producer of farmed salmon.[42] Health experts worry that such abuse of antibiotics in the aquaculture sector will reduce their effectiveness in the treatment of human diseases.[43] In addition, transporting species can introduce new diseases to native fish stocks, and in some cases escaped aquaculture species can outcompete native species.[44] Finally, as the market for carnivorous farmed fish continues to grow, more wild fish stocks are being depleted to provide fishmeal and fish oil needed for the fish farms.[45]

One way to address some of these concerns is through integrated multitrophic aquaculture.[46] For example, Egypt has developed an experimental farm in Wadi Natroun that uses a closed-loop water and nutrient system that moves water from tilapia ponds to catfish ponds and then to alfalfa fields. In addition to the circulation of nutrients through the process, the final step provides feedstock for livestock, which then produce manure that can be used to make biogas fuel. This fuel can is used to raise the water temperature for the tilapia hatcheries or to heat ponds during the winter.[47]

Choosing to farm species that perform a variety of ecosystem services can also help make aquaculture more environmentally sustainable while providing innovative solutions to water

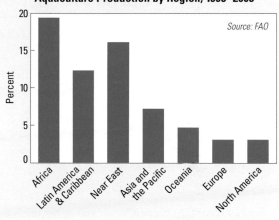

Figure 3. Average Annual Growth Rate for World Aquaculture Production by Region, 1995–2005

Source: FAO

quality, waste, and pollution problems.[48] Farming herbaceous fish provides nutrition without large carbon emissions and can help prevent eutrophication or nutrient pollution.[49] Raising filter-feeding shellfish, such as mussels, clams, and oysters, can maintain coastal water quality, while culturing aquatic plants help reduce pollution and eliminate urban waste.[50]

Given the importance of fisheries and aquaculture as a means of providing livelihoods and nutrition, governments, donor organizations, and foundations should help support the development of the fishing industry. In Uganda, the Uganda Fisheries & Fish Conservation Association lobbies the government to provide a voice to marginalized fishers—especially the women.[51] Across Africa, the International Fund for Agricultural Development is helping to build infrastructure and intersectoral management capacities as a means of fostering rural development through fisheries.[52] Despite their informal, small-scale nature and geographical remoteness, many capture fisheries and aquaculture farms provide a cornerstone for food security and economic growth in their regions—making it crucial that their sustainable development not be overlooked.

Stephanie Pappas was an intern at Worldwatch Institute.

Cocoa Production Continues Growth

Alice McKeown Jaspersen

Farmers around the world produced more than 4.3 million tons of cocoa in 2008, the latest year with data available, a growth of more than 3.6 percent over the year before.[1] Production has increased some 44 percent over the last 10 years.[2] (See Figure 1.) The amount of land dedicated to cocoa harvests declined slightly in 2008 to 8.1 million hectares, but total area has increased nearly 25 percent in the last decade.[3] (See Figure 2.)

Cocoa production is confined to rainy, tropical equatorial locations within 20 degrees of the equator.[4] Cocoa is used predominantly as a food product (such as chocolate and cocoa powder), although it is also used in cosmetics and other products.[5]

Africa dominates cocoa production, and Western Africa alone produced some 62 percent of the global crop in 2008.[6] Within the region, Côte d'Ivoire and Ghana are the leaders, at 32 percent and 16 percent of global production respectively.[7] (See Table 1.)

Asia is the next largest region of cocoa growth and was responsible for nearly 20 percent of the global crop in 2008.[8] Indonesia is by far the largest producer in the region and ranks second in terms of world production.[9] Asia showed the strongest growth in annual production increases of all regions from 2007 to 2008, at over 6 percent.[10]

The Americas follows in production quantity, with nearly 12 percent of global output of cocoa, led by Brazil, Ecuador, and Colombia, all of which were top 10 producers in 2008.[11] Growth in this region was markedly slower over the past 10 years than elsewhere—at a mere 5 percent—though the growth in 2008 over 2007 reached nearly 3.5 percent (second only to Asia).[12]

The smallest cocoa-growing region in 2008 was Oceania, which accounted for just over 1 percent of production.[13] Papua New Guinea is the predominant grower there.[14]

In Côte d'Ivoire, cocoa production has been declining partially as a result of aging trees that are less productive and more susceptible to disease (new trees only become productive when they are four or five years old).[15] Problems here

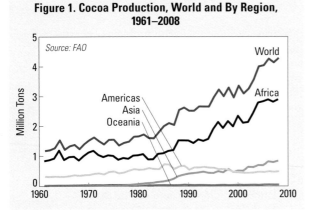

Figure 1. Cocoa Production, World and By Region, 1961–2008

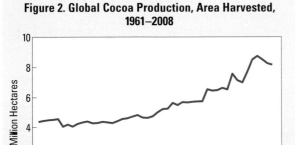

Figure 2. Global Cocoa Production, Area Harvested, 1961–2008

and in other places have increased concerns about the long-term availability of cocoa. As a result, researchers have begun looking to less traditional areas, including Vietnam and the Philippines, for cocoa expansion.[16] The International Cocoa Organization, established in 1973 by the United Nations, projects that the greatest growth in cocoa production over the next five years will be in the Americas, with production in the Dominican Republic expected to grow by 27 percent.[17] In Africa, Ghana is projected to lead in growth, with 18 percent, while Malaysia leads Asia and Oceania, with 11 percent.[18]

The supply of cocoa, weather conditions, stockpiles, and speculation about future availability directly affect the cost of cocoa on the international market. The price of cocoa beans has been rising steadily since 2006, increasing by 105 percent between January 2007 and December 2009.[19] (See Figure 3.) In December 2009 the price was 42 percent higher than a year earlier, and recent market indicators point to a relatively high price over the near term, especially as indicators show moisture issues and as viral disease may affect production in West Africa.[20]

Cocoa trade includes cocoa beans as well as processed products like cocoa powder and cocoa paste. The total export value of cocoa production is estimated to reach $10 billion in the 2009/2010 crop year.[21] In terms of cocoa beans, the Netherlands is the largest importer, as it operates a large port servicing Europe.[22] The Dutch imported some $912 million worth of beans in 2008.[23] The United States led imports of cocoa powder, which is destined for processed food products, at $98 million in 2008.[24]

One reaction to higher prices has been an increase in the production and use of cocoa butter equivalents (CBEs), which rely on fats and oils like shea and palm.[25] CBEs can offer cost savings, especially for use in the European Union, which allows products to replace up to 5 percent of their cocoa butter with substitutes and still be labeled as chocolate.[26] (But some places, including the United States, ban this practice).[27] Other companies have changed

Table 1. Top 10 Cocoa Producing Countries, 2008

Country	1999	2007	2008	Share of 2008 World Harvest
	(tons)	(tons)	(tons)	(percent)
Côte d'Ivoire	1,163,025	1,384,000	1,370,000	32
Indonesia	367,475	740,006	792,761	18
Ghana	434,200	615,000	700,000	16
Nigeria	225,000	500,000	500,000	12
Brazil	205,003	201,651	208,386	5
Cameroon	116,000	179,239	187,532	4
Ecuador	94,687	85,891	94,300	2
Togo	7,000	78,000	80,000	2
Papua New Guinea	35,600	47,300	48,800	1
Colombia	51,485	39,904	44,740	1
World Total	2,975,516	4,150,047	4,300,205	–

Source: FAOSTAT, updated 16 December 2009.

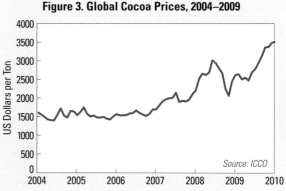

Figure 3. Global Cocoa Prices, 2004–2009

Source: ICCO

their recipes to reduce cocoa content.[28]

About 60 percent of the global chocolate and confectionary market is shared by six producers: Mars, Nestlé, Cadbury, Kraft, Ferrero, and Hershey.[29] The industry has become increasingly consolidated over the past years through mergers and acquisitions, which are expected to continue.[30]

Despite the global recession, growth in chocolate sales continued in 2009 and was up

5.9 percent in the United Kingdom, 2.6 percent in the United States, 3.2 percent in Belgium, and 18 percent in China.[31] Although chocolate is expected to remain the fastest-growing confectionery in the years to come, the pace of growth in sales is expected to drop from the 19 percent seen between 2004 and 2008 to some 15 percent between 2009 and 2013.[32] Some of the strongest growth rates are expected in Central Eastern Europe as companies continue to relocate from Western Europe to take advantage of cheaper labor markets—and in the process encourage local sales of chocolate.[33] Strong growth is also expected in emerging markets with growing consumer income, such as India, Indonesia, China, Argentina, and Brazil.[34]

People in Europe consume the most cocoa: on average more than 2 kilograms per person per year (compared with a 0.57 kilogram world average).[35] Switzerland leads overall, with 5.1 kilograms; outside of Europe, the United States consumes 2.6 kilograms per person and Canada 2.2.[36] The lowest consumption rates are generally found in Africa and in developing countries.[37] Consumption of chocolate confectionary, which is the largest end-use of cocoa, generally follows these trends, with Europe showing the highest rates: several countries are above 8 kilograms per person, compared with 5.18 kilograms in the United States.[38]

Demand and supply of cocoa can be measured in yearly grindings of the beans as they are processed into end products. Geographically, Europe generally accounts for some 41 percent of grindings, the Americas 23 percent, Asia and Oceana 20 percent, and Africa 17 percent.[39] Both global grindings and end-of-season stocks have risen over the past 10 years, although there have been yearly fluctuations.[40] (See Figures 4 and 5.)

Cocoa is largely grown on small farms (typically less than five hectares), which account for more than 90 percent of all production.[41] Small farmers can face challenges not experienced by large agribusiness, including lack of access to production research to improve farming efficiency and maximize production.[42] The World

Cocoa Foundation estimates that there are 5–6 million cocoa farmers worldwide and that cocoa production affects the livelihoods of 40–50 million people.[43]

Cocoa production can cause environmental damage, especially when pesticides and fertilizers are used and lead to water pollution and human toxicity issues.[44] Clearing forestland for cocoa is another concern and can cause biodiversity loss and soil nutrient depletion.[45]

Reports of widespread child labor in West Africa for cocoa production surfaced in 2000, leading to the Harkin-Engel Protocol.[46] This is a voluntary collaboration by chocolate manufacturers, governments, and nongovernmental organizations to eliminate the worst forms of child labor.[47] Recent reports show that child trafficking and labor for cocoa farming is still prevalent in Côte d'Ivoire—earlier estimates showed that at least 109,000 children were working in hazardous conditions in the production of cocoa—and estimates indicate that some 24 percent of children between the ages of 5 and 17 in cocoa-growing regions there have worked on a cocoa farm within the past year.[48] Children as young as five work in cocoa in Ghana and Côte d'Ivoire, and a significant number of them are involved in hazardous work or have been injured.[49]

In addition to reducing child labor, some organizations and cocoa producers have launched efforts to address other sustainability issues. The International Cocoa Organization originally focused on price supports, but in 2001 its mission shifted to creating a sustainable cocoa economy.[50] Cargill Cocoa & Chocolate operates Farmer Field Schools in Côte d'Ivoire to train local farmers and estimates that its program can increase income by 30 percent through increased yields and better quality.[51] The World Cocoa Foundation works through Farmer Field Schools and other methods to improve pest and disease management, diversify farm income, strengthen farmer organizations, and train farmers on improved production methods.[52] The Foundation has also targeted women farmers through novel approaches like a Video Viewing Club that teaches women through videos, manuals, discussion groups, and hands-on training activities about responses to pests and diseases and about proper production and post-harvest methods.[53]

Another way to address sustainability issues has been the development of specialized products for the consumer market that are linked to changes in production. Fair trade and organic chocolate products are on the rise, a trend that is expected to continue.[54] Global fair trade sales of chocolate increased 35 percent in 2009, with sales rising both in traditional strongholds like the United Kingdom and the United States and in emerging markets.[55] Cocoa products with a fair trade label follow regulations that set minimum prices for cocoa beans and establish some social and environmental standards. Growth in organic certification, seen as a potential response to environmental concerns, also remained strong.[56]

Negotiations on the seventh International Cocoa Agreement concluded in June 2010, with the pact to take effect in 2012.[57] Unlike previous versions, the new agreement will be in place for a minimum of 10 years.[58] Representing a cooperative agreement between cocoa importers and producers, the pact aims to increase the income of cocoa farmers in order to make production more equitable and fair.[59] The agreement also reinforces a longer-term commitment to establish a sustainable cocoa economy.[60]

Alice McKeown Jaspersen was the director of Vital Signs Online.

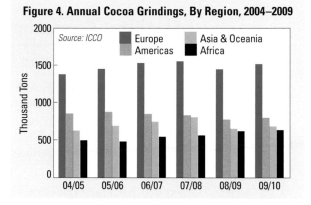

Figure 4. Annual Cocoa Grindings, By Region, 2004–2009

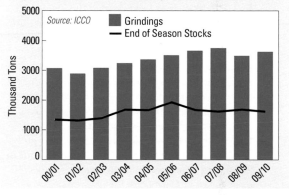

Figure 5. Global Cocoa Grindings and Stocks, 2000–2009

Fertilizer Consumption Declines Sharply

Matt Styslinger

Global consumption of inorganic fertilizers fell 7.5 percent to 156 million tons in 2008, the sharpest one-year decline in nearly half a century of data collection.[1] (See Figure 1.) The decline was a direct response to price spikes in 2007 and 2008 that caused demand to fall.

Demand for fertilizer had been expanding rapidly over the last decade, driven by growing demand for crops used to produce biofuels and to raise livestock, which drove fertilizer prices in April 2008 to at least double the levels of a year earlier.[2] Farmers were unable or unwilling to pay that much, and consumption is believed to have dropped 1–5 percent in 2009.[3] The global credit collapse, trade recession, and slowing of world economic growth further reduced demand, which in turn caused fertilizer prices to drop dramatically to pre-2007 levels. Now farmers have begun to restock their inventories.[4] Early indications show that global demand for fertilizer has grown by 4 percent in 2010, and sustained growth rates are expected over the next four years.[5]

Fertilizer increases agricultural yields and is now used in the production of 40–60 percent of the world's food supply.[6] Inorganic fertilizer (also called chemical fertilizer, commercial fertilizer, or artificial fertilizer)—the chief source of added nutrients in commercial agriculture today—is manufactured through the crushing of minerals, mechanical enrichment, or chemical transformation of raw materials.[7] It contains three major nutrients—nitrogen, phosphorus, and potash—but unlike manures and other organic fertilizers, it lacks the organic matter and other ingredients that build soil structure and contribute to soil health. And it carries substantial environmental risk, especially as a water pollutant.

During the 2008–09 drop in fertilizer consumption, South Asia's use actually grew by around 7.4 percent.[8] Usage in East Asia, in contrast, dropped 5.9 percent in the same period.[9] East Asia accounts for 38.3 percent of consumption, while South Asia uses 19.6 percent of the world's artificial fertilizers.[10] (See Figure 2.) According to the U.N. Food and Agriculture Organization, in the next two years East Asia and South Asia together will account for over half of the total growth of global fertilizer use.[11] The need to improve crop productivity to feed a fast-growing population is driving this trend. Although there has been significant loss of arable land due to rapid urbanization, agricultural production has increased steadily throughout Asia.[12]

In North America, fertilizer consumption dropped 15.1 percent in 2008–09.[13] Although crop production has increased rapidly due to bioethanol production, gains in nitrogen use efficiency and greater recycling of organic nutrients is tempering fertilizer demands.[14] The four major U.S. crops—corn, cotton, soybeans, and wheat—account for about 60 percent of crop

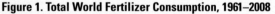

Figure 1. Total World Fertilizer Consumption, 1961–2008

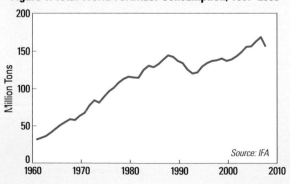

Source: IFA

acreage and receive over 60 percent of the nitrogen, phosphate, and potash used in the United States.[15]

In Western and Central Europe, fertilizer use dropped 23.9 percent during the global dip in 2008–09, while consumption in Eastern Europe and Central Asia actually rose marginally.[16] Over the next two years, usage in these regions is expected to grow only fractionally at a rate of 0.6 percent. This is largely due to environmental regulations on water, air, and soil quality in Western Europe. In addition, nutrient budgeting and mandates on greater recycling of organic nutrients are being implemented. These factors are likely to constrain use of artificial fertilizers in Western Europe in the near future.[17] And although some growth is expected over the next two years in Eastern Europe and Central Asia, poor economic structure and performance will likely hold growth back there.[18]

In other regions, Latin America's fertilizer consumption dropped some 14.1 percent in the 2008–09 decline, Oceania's consumption dropped 13.9 percent, and Africa's dropped by 2.3 percent.[19] Much of Latin America's expected growth in consumption will continue to take place in Brazil and Argentina, whose farmers are working to meet increased demand for sugarcane ethanol.[20] Severe drought in recent years in Australia, lack of agricultural subsidies there and in New Zealand, and unfavorable currency exchange rates have all affected demand for fertilizer in Oceania, limiting the expected growth in the rate of consumption over the next two years to 3.9 percent.[21]

The value of total global agricultural output (food, non-food, and livestock commodities) has more than doubled since 1961, and it will need to increase by about 40 percent by 2030 and 70 percent by 2050 if it is to meet growing demands for food.[22] Some 90 percent of the growth in crop production—80 percent of which will be in developing countries—is likely to come from increased cropping intensity and fertilizer use. The rest of the growth will come from land expansion.[23]

Population growth and changing diets asso-

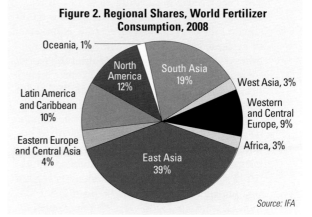

Figure 2. Regional Shares, World Fertilizer Consumption, 2008

Source: IFA

ciated with increased wealth in Asia suggest that global demand for meat could increase there by more than 50 percent by 2030, boosting the demand for fertilizer to produce feed.[24] Already an estimated 80 percent of global soybean production and 40 percent of corn goes to feeding animals.[25]

Biofuel production has risen sharply, increasing the demand for energy crops and the consequent demand for fertilizers.[26] U.S. farmers planted approximately 85 million acres of corn in 2009–10—the third largest acreage since 1949 (following 2007 and 2008).[27] As much as one third of this will be used to produce ethanol.[28] In Brazil, the production of sugarcane and soybeans—the primary feedstocks for biofuel production—is expected to grow 12 percent and 34 percent, respectively, in 2011 from 2006 levels.[29] For the world as a whole, some 2.4 percent of total global fertilizer consumption in 2012 is projected to be for biofuel production.[30]

Heavy fertilizer use, particularly of phosphorus and nitrogen fertilizers, is a major contributor to eutrophication—the addition of high concentrations of nutrients—in rivers, lakes, and coastal waters.[31] Nutrient runoff from industrial agricultural activity—including misuse and overuse of fertilizers and manure from factory farms—stimulates overgrowth of algae that consumes oxygen in the water, creating "dead zones" that are devoid of aquatic life.[32]

The average size of the dead zone area in the Gulf of Mexico over the past five years is 6,000 square miles.[33] The 2010 dead zone is projected to measure between 6,500 and 7,800 square miles—as big as New Jersey. Around the world, there are nearly 400 similar dead zones, including along the coasts of China, Japan, and southeast Australia.[34]

Supplies of the ingredients of fertilizers may be a cause for concern. About 90 percent of phosphorus reserves are found in only five countries: the United States, China, Morocco, South Africa, and Jordan.[35] And some analysts suggest that phosphorus supply will be insufficient to meet demand in 30–40 years.[36] A September 2010 report by the International Fertilizer Development Center disputes those shortage claims and estimates phosphate reserves are sufficient to supply fertilizer for 300–400 years.[37]

A recent National Research Council report suggests that increasingly popular sustainable agricultural approaches could reduce reliance on chemical inputs.[38] Practices like crop rotation, intercropping, cultivar mixtures, and management of non-crop vegetation contribute to the resilience of farming systems. Meanwhile, natural nutrient management, including the use of legumes, animal manure, and compost, along with natural soil management—using conservation tillage and cover crops—can improve soil quality and crop yields, reducing the need for artificial fertilizers.

Biochar is another innovation that could help curb the growth of inorganic fertilizer use. The biochar process converts agricultural waste into a porous charcoal that helps soils retain nutrients, agrochemicals, and water, reducing the need for chemical inputs. This also improves water quality, as more nutrients stay in the soil instead of leaching into groundwater. The use of biochar has been endorsed by many national governments and by the United Nations Convention to Combat Desertification as a promising tool to mitigate climate change.[39]

Matt Styslinger is an intern at Worldwatch Institute.

Global Economy and Resources Trends

NASA/GSFC/METI/ERSDAC/JAROS, and US/Japan ASTER Science Team

Ore from the Escondida open-pit mine in Chile yields copper, silver, and gold.

For additional global economy and resources trends, go to vitalsigns.worldwatch.org.

Global Output Stagnant

Gary Gardner

The gross world product increased by just 0.3 percent in 2009 as the Great Recession took hold in many of the world's economies.[1] (See Figure 1.) The anemic increase was a sharp slowdown from the 2000–08 period, when global output increased 6.6 percent annually.[2] World output is expected to have recovered somewhat in 2010, with growth estimated at roughly 4 percent.[3]

Gross world product measures the output of goods and services for the world economy as a whole. It is commonly broken into consumption, investment, and government spending. The data presented here are calculated based on the purchasing power parity exchange rate, which converts national output to a common currency that reflects equivalent purchasing power across countries.[4]

Growth differed markedly by region and economy. Advanced economies actually shrank by 2 percent in 2009, while emerging and developing economies continued to grow—albeit slowly compared with earlier years—at 3.3 percent.[5] (See Table 1.) Some of the largest emerging economies grew at very high rates: China's economy, for example, grew at 9.1 percent in 2009 and India's at 7.4 percent.[6]

Trade volumes were also off sharply in 2009, declining by 10.7 percent.[7] As with economic growth overall, developing countries fared best. Imports in industrial countries fell by 12 percent in 2009 but by 8.4 percent in developing and emerging countries.[8] Exports from industrial countries declined by 11.7 percent compared with 8.2 percent from developing and emerging economies.[9] Developing-country performance is especially notable in the face of declining prices in 2009 for many commodities, the engines of growth for many developing economies. Oil prices fell by some 36.3 percent, and non-fuel commodity prices were off by 18.7 percent.[10]

Unemployment increased in all advanced countries in 2009, with Spain, Ireland, and the Slovak Republic registering unemployment rates of greater than 10 percent.[11] But some advanced countries fared better. Austria, the Netherlands, Switzerland, Norway, Denmark, South Korea, and Singapore all kept unemployment rates in 2009 to less than 5 percent.[12]

The International Monetary Fund credits three developments with preventing the Great Recession from being even worse than it was. First, stimulus packages were engineered in many industrial countries that kept demand from falling through the floor. Second, recovery of the financial sector in many countries proceeded faster than expected. And third, firms stopped liquidating inventories; many companies, fearing that another Great Depression might materialize, liquidated inventories in late 2008 and early 2009 to avoid being stuck with unmovable stocks of goods and to raise cash. Rebuilding these inventories has been a spur to growth in many economies.[13]

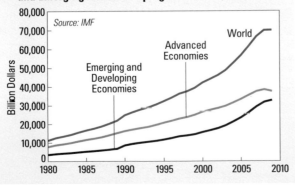

Figure 1. Gross Product: World, Advanced Economies, and Emerging and Developing Economies, 1980–2009

Table 1. Economic Growth, 2009, Selected Regions and Economic Blocs

Region or Economic Bloc	Growth rate, 2009
	(percent)
Advanced economies	
Group of 7	−2.30
European Union	−3.00
Other advanced economies	−0.02
Developing and Emerging Economies	
Central and Eastern Europe	−2.72
Former Soviet Union and Soviet states	−5.75
Developing Asia	7.80
Middle East and North Africa	3.58
Sub-Saharan Africa	3.17
Latin America and Caribbean	−0.71

Source: IMF, World Economic Database, *April 2010.*

Table 2. Green Stimulus Packages, Various Countries, 2009

Country	Stimulus	Green Stimulus	Green Share
	(billion dollars)		(percent)
Australia	26.7	2.5	9.4
United Kingdom	30.4	2.1	6.9
Canada	31.8	2.6	8.2
France	33.7	7.1	21.1
South Korea	38.1	30.7	80.6
Italy	103.5	1.3	1.3
Germany	104.8	13.8	13.2
Japan	485.9	12.4	2.6
China	586.1	221.3	37.8
United States	787.0	94.1	12.0

Source: World Bank, World Development Report 2010, (Washington, DC: 2010) p. 59.

Economic ministers worldwide are challenged to reconcile two competing outcomes of economic growth. On one hand, economic expansion generates jobs, along with the well-being and opportunity that stable employment can bring—especially if jobs are high quality with good pay. At the same time, growth in modern industrial economies typically drives up the use of materials and fuel, both of which can be harmful to the environment. Waste of all kinds, from carbon emissions to municipal solid waste, has tended to increase historically with economic growth.[14] And resources are also rendered scarce with growth, as shortages of water, minerals, and fuels make clear.

To reduce waste and pressure on resources, some governments are working to green their economies. In 2009, a key policy tool used for this purpose was green stimulus packages, which aimed to boost economic activity in a sustainable way, especially through infrastructure investments. At the global level, some 11–16 percent of stimulus packages were green, depending on the definition of green used.[15] At the national level, the green share of stimulus packages varied greatly, from a few percentage points in many countries to some 81 percent in South Korea.[16] (See Table 2.) Most green stimulus spending globally went to rail, modernized electricity grids, and investments in building efficiency.[17] Less than a quarter of all green stimulus spending approved in 2009 was spent that year, with the bulk planned for disbursement in 2010 and 2011.[18]

Other governments look to long-term economic restructuring to reconcile the job creation and pollution-generating consequences of growth. They are working to decouple economic growth from materials and energy use, creating "circular economies" that promote the reduction, recycling, and reuse of materials. Germany, Japan, and China are leaders in the field, with Japan having perhaps the most extensive measurable impact to date. A law passed in 2000 established goals for 2010: to increase resource productivity by 60 percent and recycling by 40–50 percent and to reduce waste disposal by 60 percent.[19] As of 2008, Japan was estimated to be on track to meet its goals:[20] resource productivity had increased by 37 percent, municipal waste levels were down by 40 percent, and disposal of non-municipal waste was down by 55 percent.[21] China has also begun work on development of a circular economy, launching a set of pilot projects in 2005 in seven key industrial sectors in 10 provinces or cities, an effort that was expanded in 2007 and 2008.[22] China has also developed an experimental Circular Economy Evaluation Indicators System with two types of indicators—some at the level of the industrial park and a second set at a more macro level.[23]

At the same time, some government are working to redefine the very purpose of economies and embracing economic measures that focus on the delivery of well-being rather than on economic output. A 2010 report from the Wuppertal Institute identifies three major national efforts to adjust gross domestic product (GDP) (such as green GDP or Green National Accounting), five to replace it (such as the Human Development Index or the Ecological Footprint), and eight to supplement it (such as the Millennium Development Goals).[24] France, the United Kingdom, and Austria are in various stages of studying alternative measures of economic progress, as are the European Union and the Organisation for Economic Co-operation and Development.[25] China, after adopting and then abandoning a green GDP measure in 2005, embraced a new plan in 2010 based on 55 indicators—from carbon emissions per person to the share of environmental spending in the government budget.[26] And in November 2010 the United Kingdom unveiled plans to launch a Happiness Index that will serve as a complement to GDP as a measure of national progress.[27]

Unemployment and Precarious Employment Grow More Prominent

Michael Renner

After declining from 2004 to 2007, global unemployment took an upturn in 2008 and then sharply rose to 212 million in 2009.[1] For mid-2010, the International Labour Organization (ILO) estimates that 210 million people were unemployed.[2] This compares with a range of 170–190 million jobless persons during the previous decade.[3] The global unemployment rate rose from 5.7 percent in 2007 to 6.6 percent in 2009.[4] (See Table 1.)

The total number of people with employment worldwide did rise—from about 2.6 billion in 1999 to roughly 3 billion in 2009—but not enough to keep pace with the growth in the working-age population.[5]

Governments took a range of steps to counter the impacts of the recent economic crisis, including stimulus packages, job retention measures, and increased reliance on part-time employment. These measures are estimated to have either saved or created some 20 million jobs worldwide.[6] Despite such efforts, industrial economies suffered a jump in the unemployment rate of 2.4 percentage points from 2007 to 2009, followed by the countries in Europe that do not belong to the European Union and by the former Soviet Union (2.0 points) and then by Latin America and the Caribbean (1.2 points).[7] Other parts of the world saw more limited increases in unemployment rates (0.5 points or less).[8]

Although there are signs that the world economy is once more growing, employment trends in many countries are lagging badly—especially when the growth in the working-age population is taken into account. Indeed, in advanced economies where job growth has remained weak, more than 14 million jobs are needed to restore the employment-to-population ratio to pre-crisis levels.[9] (See Table 2.) Even in emerging economies where employment growth has been much stronger, a recovery to pre-crisis employment rates is unlikely in the medium term.[10]

Table 1. Unemployment Rates, World and Regions, 1999 and 2004–2009

Region	1999	2004	2005	2006	2007	2008	2009
Industrial economies	7.0	7.2	6.9	6.3	5.7	6.0	8.4
Non-EU Europe and former Soviet Union	12.4	9.7	9.4	9.0	8.3	8.3	10.3
East Asia	4.7	4.2	4.2	4.0	3.8	4.3	4.4
Southeast Asia and Pacific	5.1	6.4	6.5	6.1	5.4	5.3	5.6
South Asia	4.3	5.2	5.3	5.1	5.0	4.8	5.1
Latin America and Caribbean	8.5	8.4	8.0	7.4	7.0	7.0	8.2
Middle East	9.3	9.3	10.0	9.5	9.3	9.2	9.4
North Africa	13.1	12.3	11.5	10.4	10.1	10.0	10.5
Sub-Saharan Africa	8.2	8.2	8.2	8.2	8.0	8.0	8.2
World	6.4	6.4	6.3	6.0	5.7	5.8	6.6

Source: ILO, Global Employment Trends January 2010 *(Geneva: 2010).*

Table 2. Jobs Needed to Return to Pre-crisis Employment Rates

	Employment Rate Gap
	(million jobs)
Industrial countries	14.3
Africa	1.2
Asia and the Pacific	1.6
Central and Eastern Europe and former Soviet Republics	3.5
Latin America and the Caribbean	2.1
World	22.7

Source: International Institute for Labour Studies, World of Work Report 2010 (Geneva: ILO, 2010).

In South Asia, Latin America and the Caribbean, and the Middle East and North Africa, as well as in industrial economies, female unemployment increased more than male unemployment did.[11] Only in Central and Southeastern Europe as well as in the successor states of the former Soviet Union did women fare better than men.[12]

Even before the current crisis, young people—defined as persons between 15 and 24 years of age—were almost three times as likely as adults to be unemployed.[13] In 2009, the global youth unemployment rate rose to 13.4 percent, affecting an additional 8.5 million people.[14] (See Figure 1.) Most of this job loss occurred in industrial economies. The highest unemployment rates for young people are found in the Middle East and North Africa.[15]

Unemployment statistics do not include so-called discouraged persons—those who are available for work but do not actively seek it because of poor job prospects. In addition, as the ILO explains, discouragement "may also result in decisions to postpone labor market entry, in particular by youth, or to withdraw from the labor force and retire."[16] By the end of 2009, more than 4 million job seekers had stopped looking for work in countries for which information is available.[17]

Having a job is important, yet some 1.5 bil-

lion persons are in highly vulnerable employment situations.[18] The conditions they face include inadequate earnings, low-productivity work, and jobs that violate or undermine the fundamental rights of workers. The ILO notes that the share of employment that is vulnerable had been on a downward trend (from more than 53 percent in 1999 to 49.5 percent in 2008), but that was halted by the crisis.[19]

A related category is that of the "working poor." Although the figure had decreased during the past decade, the share of employed people who fall in the extreme working poor category (earning less than $1.25 per day) worldwide was still more than 21 per cent in 2008, or 632 million workers.[20] And the total rose to an estimated 744 million people in 2009.[21] Those earning $2 a day or less accounted for almost 40 percent of the global workforce, or 1,187 million workers, in 2008.[22] Their ranks rose to an estimated 45.6 percent, or 1,283 million people, in 2009.[23] A good number of these individuals live in South Asia. (See Figure 2.)

Rich countries are faced with the rise of precarious employment—with little job and income security for affected workers. Although the wages of these individuals are too high to be included in the statistics just cited, relative to the cost of living their earnings are often barely enough to make ends meet.

Outsourcing of jobs to lower-wage countries, including the rapidly rising economies of China and India, has led to job loss and to downward pressure on wages. Initially limited to lower-skilled occupations, outsourcing is increasingly affecting higher-skilled jobs as well. Governments in many industrial countries are not investing enough in mitigating programs, such as minimum wage requirements, ameliorative social programs, or adequate education and worker retraining initiatives.[24]

In the United States, wage stagnation and growing income inequality have been prominent phenomena since the late 1970s. More than a quarter of all U.S. workers earned poverty-level hourly wages in 2007.[25] Inflation-adjusted average hourly earnings were slightly above $17 in

1978, a level not seen again until 2002 despite ongoing productivity gains, which are typically seen as permitting wage increases.[26] In 2000–06, for example, median real wages grew by 0.3 percent a year, considerably outpaced by annual labor productivity growth of 2.5 percent.[27] During the last two decades, wages have lagged behind productivity gains in many other countries as well.[28]

In 2009–10, U.S. unemployment hovered between 9 and 10 percent, afflicting close to 15 million people by the end of 2010.[29] In addition, more than 6 million people have been unable to find work and have stopped looking.[30]

Particularly troublesome for the United States has been the decline of employment in manufacturing industries, which typically offer the best-paying jobs for blue-collar workers. In the last decade, manufacturing jobs declined from 17.3 million in 2000 to almost 14 million in 2007 (the last full year prior to the current economic recession) and to 11.6 million for the first nine months of 2010.[31]

In Europe's largest economy, Germany, unemployment is at just above 7 percent in 2010, below the rates prevalent in other major European economies: 7.8 percent in the United Kingdom, 8.4 percent in Italy, and 9.8 percent in France.[32] But Germany's low-wage sector (defined as two thirds of the median hourly wage or less) has grown rapidly—from 15 percent of all employees in 1995 to 21 percent in 2008.[33] Unlike France or the United States, Germany does not have any minimum wage standards, and a growing share of low-wage employees receive less than half the median wage.[34]

The absolute number of German low-wage workers—including many full-time and skilled persons—grew from 4.3 million in 1998 to 6.6 million in 2008.[35] Among them, 1.3 million workers depend on welfare programs to make ends meet.[36]

Income polarization between rich and poor German households reached new highs following years of weak or negative employment growth in 1993–94 and in 2003–05. But even when the economy expanded in 1998–2000 and

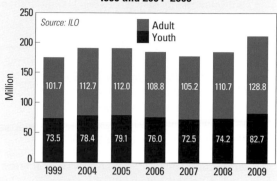

Figure 1. Global Unemployment, Adult and Youth, 1999 and 2004–2009

Source: ILO

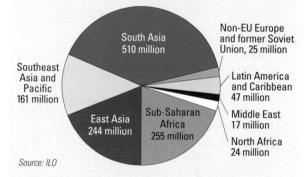

Figure 2. People Earning $2 or Less per Day, 2009

South Asia 510 million

Non-EU Europe and former Soviet Union, 25 million

Southeast Asia and Pacific 161 million

Latin America and Caribbean 47 million

East Asia 244 million

Sub-Saharan Africa 255 million

Middle East 17 million

North Africa 24 million

Source: ILO

2007–08, polarization did not recede.[37] Income disparities have also translated into lopsided wealth distribution. In 2007, the richest 1 percent of Germans controlled 23 percent of the wealth and the top 10 percent had 61 percent.[38] The bottom 70 percent had just 9 percent.[39]

In Japan, the mid-2010 unemployment rate stood at 5.1 percent—lower than in most other industrial countries but much higher than the 1–3 percent range prevalent from the late 1960s to the mid-1990s.[40] Some 20 million part-time and contract workers in Japan lack job security today and do not receive decent wages and benefits.[41] They account for 34 percent of the country's total labor force, up from less than 20 percent in 1990.[42]

The number of Japanese workers who earned less than the official poverty line (which is set at about half the median wage) reached more than 10 million in 2006, an increase of 30 percent over the previous decade.[43] At the same time, the social safety net has been pared back since the late 1990s. Today, close to 16 percent of the Japanese population lives in relative poverty.[44]

In rich countries, growing phenomena like long-term unemployment, low-wage employment, and the emergence of a permanent underclass bode ill for social cohesion and ultimately the social peace. They could also translate into the political sphere in troubling ways, either by reinforcing political apathy or by increasing the attraction of extremist political ideas.

Western industrial countries and Japan are increasingly being challenged by the tremendous rise of economies like China, India, and others. Yet wages in China are still low and remain subdued even as its economy recovers from the impacts of the global recession. Wages in China accounted for less than 40 percent of the country's gross domestic product (GDP) in 2007, down from 52 percent in 2000.[45] (By contrast, wages account for roughly two thirds of GDP in western industrial countries.) Productivity gains have not benefited the majority of the country's workers, and inequality has increased.[46]

Low wages and weak social safety nets (which compel households to build precautionary savings) limit domestic demand in emerging economies. Thus their economic growth is driven to a considerable extent by exports to western industrialized countries—countries that, due to wage stagnation, have financed their consumption through a buildup of debt.[47] The underlying imbalances continue to plague the world economy and could lead to growing frictions over trade, exchange rates, and other economic policies, all of which affect employment prospects.

I would like to thank Raymond Torres and Steven Tobin of the International Labour Organization for their valuable feedback on an earlier draft.

Materials Use Up

Gary Gardner

Global use of materials—the food, feed, forest products, metals, and minerals that constitute the foundation of modern economies—was up 2.7 percent in 2007, the latest year for which global data are available.[1] (See Figure 1.) The 2007 pre-recession expansion was the fifth consecutive year of relatively robust global growth in materials use.[2]

Materials in the global economy broadly consist of two types: nonrenewables, which include construction minerals, industrial minerals, and metals, and renewables, typically the biomass harvested for feed, food, and forestry as well as animal products. (As defined here, materials do not include water, fossil fuels, or "unused" materials associated with extraction, such as the earth that is moved to get to mining ores or soils eroded in agricultural production.) Nonrenewables extraction was up 3.2 percent in 2007, while biomass extraction increased 1.9 percent.[3]

Materials use is a proxy indicator for environmental impact: the greater the tonnage of virgin materials extracted, processed, consumed, and disposed of, the greater an economy's environmental footprint. (The impact of one key set of materials—toxic substances such as mercury or cadmium—is often understated by tonnage measurements, however. A ton of mercury, for example, could have much greater environmental or human impact than a ton of iron ore or timber.)

Because materials use in modern economies is closely connected to economic growth, usage by region reflects regional economic trends. Emerging economies saw the greatest increases in total materials use in 2007 relative to both 2006 and 2000, with Asia and Latin America reporting particularly robust rates of growth.[4] (See Table 1.) Industrial countries, with largely completed infrastructures and mature countries,

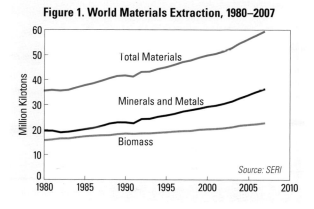

Figure 1. World Materials Extraction, 1980–2007

saw much more modest rates of growth. Africa's largely nonindustrial economies also experienced modest growth.

Materials use tends to increase as nations industrialize. Total materials use globally increased from 7 billion tons in 1900 to about 60 billion tons in 2006, and use per person dou-

Table 1. Regional Change in Total 2007 Materials Use

Region	Compared with 2000	Compared with 2006
	(percent)	
Africa	19.0	1.5
Asia	31.2	5.4
Europe	3.8	–1.7
Latin America and Caribbean	23.6	4.9
North America	2.9	–1.0
Oceania	10.7	2.1
World	19.4	2.7

Source: Based on SERI, www.materialflows.net.

bled over the century, from 4.6 tons to 8–9 tons.[5] People in industrial economies use four to eight times more resources than people in predominantly agricultural societies and 15 to 30 times more than those in hunter-gatherer societies.[6] On the other hand, people in countries with high population density use fewer materials per person at the same standard of living than people in less-dense countries do.[7]

At the global level, economies have become more efficient in materials use over time, consuming around 30 percent fewer resources to produce one unit of gross domestic product than they did 30 years ago.[8] Despite this encouraging trend, global resource use rose about 50 percent over the same period, as population growth and rising prosperity drove up demand.[9] Meanwhile, the Sustainable Europe Research Institute, which follows materials trends, estimates that global resource use could increase by another two thirds by 2030.[10]

As economies grow worldwide, analysts worry that expanded materials use will create unbearable environmental pressures. Given the materials-intensive nature of most industrial economies, the projected fourfold expansion of the global economy over the next half-century or so—which implies 3 percent annual growth—would increase resource demand by fourfold as well. To reduce resource use by half in that period implies increasing resource productivity by some 6 percent a year.[11] This is a tall order: current resource productivity growth is only about 2.5 percent a year.[12]

Some analysts also see signs that materials will become scarcer. For many material resources the peak production point appears to have passed. At the same time, the ore grade of many metals is declining in quality. Copper ore in 1925, for example, had an ore grade of 25 percent but fell to 0.8 percent by 1985.[13] Mining lower-grade ores requires a great deal more energy, which could be a growing constraint to metals extraction as cheap, energy-dense resources like fossil fuels become scarcer or are too dirty to use.[14]

A 2009 study compiled, from four previous

Table 2. Common Metals and Their Estimated Availabilities

Element	Estimated Availability
	(years)
Silver	9–29
Gold	10–45
Cadmium	20–50
Cobalt	50–135
Copper	25–61
Iron	48–119
Manganese	25–50
Nickel	30–100
Lead	8–42
Tin	17–50
Zinc	10–46

Source: Wouters and Bol, Material Scarcity: An M2i Study (Netherlands: Materials Innovation Institute, 2009).

studies, estimates of the remaining availability of common metals and minerals (calculated by dividing total global reserves by rates of use). Availabilities were often measured in just a few decades.[15] (See Table 2.) The estimates might underestimate availability because they assume no improvements in technology or changes in policy. On the other hand, they might overestimate availability because they assume no increase in per person usage of the metals and minerals.

Some minerals are not scarce geologically, but restricted market access creates economic scarcity. This is true for rare earths, a group of 17 elements used in metallurgical applications, alloys, electronics, and catalytic converters; as chemical catalysts; and as phosphors for computer monitors, lighting, radar, and televisions.[16] They are also used in glass polishing and petroleum refining processes.[17] China controlled 97 percent of global rare earth production in 2009, and the country halted exports of the minerals in 2010 in response to supply and pollution issues.[18] Prices for many rare earths have more than doubled in 2010 as a result.[19]

As concern about the availability of virgin

Table 3. In-use Stocks, per Person, of Selected Metals

Metal	Global per capita stock	MDC per capita stock	LDC per capita stock
		(kilograms)	
Aluminium	80	350–500	35
Copper	35–55	140–300	30–40
Iron	2200	7,000–14,000	2,000
Lead	8	20–150	1–4
Steel		7,085	
Stainless Steel		80–180	15
Zinc		80–200	20–40

Source: Graedel, Metal Stocks in Society *(Paris: UNEP, 2010).*

stocks of materials grows, greater attention is paid to the stock of materials in use and their availability for recycling and reuse. In Japan, a 2008 presentation estimated that in-use stocks (those being used in an economy) of gold, indium, silver, tin, and tantalum were 10–20 percent of estimated virgin reserves of those metals.[20] But little is known about the quantities of in-use stocks. A 2010 study for the International Panel for Sustainable Resource Manage-

ment found that data on in-use stocks of metals and their in-use lifetimes exist only for 5 of 54 metals considered: aluminium, copper, iron, lead, and zinc.[21] (See Table 3.) And their whereabouts are known only in the most general sense: for those metals, in-use stocks per person are 5–10 times greater in industrial countries than in developing ones.[22]

Some governments and scientific organizations are working to decouple economic growth from materials use, creating "circular economies" by promoting the reduction, recycling, and reuse of materials. Germany, Japan, and China are leaders in the field, with Japan having perhaps the most extensive measurable impact to date. A law passed in 2000 established goals to increase resource productivity by 60 percent and recycling by 40–50 percent and to reduce waste disposal by 60 percent.[23] Data through 2007, the most recent available, suggest that the Japanese are succeeding: resource productivity increased by 37 percent and disposal of municipal waste fell by 40 percent while disposal of nonmunicipal waste was down by 55 percent.[24] As of 2008, Japan was estimated to be on track to meet its 2010 goals.[25]

Roundwood Production Plummets

Gary Gardner

Global roundwood production fell by more than 4 percent in 2008 to 3.45 billion cubic meters, as the global recession drove a severe slump in wood-intensive industries, especially housing.[1] (See Figure 1.) The decline was the largest percentage drop since the Food and Agriculture Organization (FAO) of the United Nations began tracking production in 1961.[2] Output fell to levels last seen in 2004.[3]

The 2008 drop in production was also large on a per capita basis, at 5 percent, in part because of the recession but also because of a long structural decline dating back to at least 1961.[4] Many economic sectors have replaced wood with other materials, and wood use has become more efficient. (See Figure 2.) In 2008, roundwood production per person worldwide was about a third smaller than in 1961.[5]

Roundwood is felled timber, and it is the broadest category of wood harvested for human ends. It consists of two major subgroups. Industrial roundwood, which accounted for 45 percent of total production in 2008, is converted to commodities such as sawnlogs, veneer logs,

pulpwood, and paper.[6] Fuelwood, the remaining 55 percent of production, is used for heating and cooking in developing countries and for heating, typically in wood stoves, in industrial countries.[7]

The largest changes in production came in the United States, which saw a decline of 13.5 percent in 2008, and in Europe, which declined by 9.2 percent.[8] (See Figure 3.) The Oceania region, by contrast, saw a large increase of more than 8 percent, while Asia and Africa saw modest increases of about 2 percent and 1 percent, respectively.[9] The longer-term trend is characterized by production decreases in North America and Asia and by increases in Oceania and Central and South America. Europe has seen mostly increases over the past decade, but the region is only now reaching the production levels of around 1990.[10]

Roundwood is economically important, although its share of global economic activity has diminished over time. The value of roundwood production increased by a modest 20 percent between 1990 and 2006, from $98 billion to $118 billion, while its contribution to the gross world product fell from 1.4 percent to 1.0 percent.[11] But an emerging structural shift in roundwood markets—especially strong demand for fuelwood, which could grow stronger if cellulosic biofuels emerge as a viable energy source—could increase the share of wood resources in the global economy.[12]

Production of roundwood has a significant environment impact on forests. Some 30 percent of the world's 3.8 billion hectares of forests is used primarily for production of wood and nonwood products, and another 24 percent is used for a variety of purposes, including wood production.[13] Some of this activity contributed to the 13 million hectares of forest lost to agricul-

Figure 1. World Roundwood Production, 1961–2008

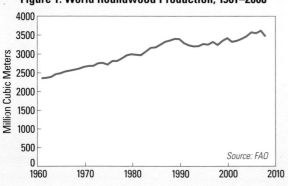

Source: FAO

ture or other economic uses, or to fire and other natural disasters, that occurred each year in the past decade.[14] At the same time, newly seeded forests in some countries reduced forest loss to a net 5.2 million hectares annually.[15] Planted area now accounts for 7 percent of the world's forested area.[16] However, some of this planted area—tree farms known as plantation forests—lacks species diversity and other ecological assets, and it cannot be considered the equivalent of a natural forest.

Roundwood is also environmentally significant because of its carbon content. FAO's *Forestry Resource Assessment 2010* estimates that the world's forests hold some 289 gigatons of carbon and that deforestation reduces this stock by about 0.5 gigatons annually.[17] Indeed, deforestation accounts for more than 17 percent of annual global greenhouse gas emissions.[18] Thus policies to reward countries for not reducing forest area, called reduced emissions from deforestation and degradation (REDD) initiatives, are under consideration internationally. But such programs face a number of challenges, including setting baseline values for forest area, ensuring that new plantings are permanently protected, and monitoring the well-being of new forested area. If REDD-like conservation initiatives gain traction in policy circles—and it is not clear that they will—it could affect roundwood production in some countries.[19]

Some production of roundwood is carried out illegally, which also has environmental consequences, including soil erosion, loss of species, and increased susceptibility to fire.[20] The extent of illegal logging is difficult to establish, not least because no common definition of the activity exists. But a 2008 paper from the Congressional Research Service estimates that as much as 23–30 percent of hardwood lumber and plywood traded globally is illegally logged.[21] For some countries, more than half of all harvesting is estimated to be illegal.[22] Russia, Indonesia, and Brazil are often mentioned as the leaders in illegal logging.

One tool to ensure legal, sustainable harvesting of roundwood is certification, a process

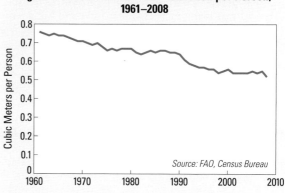

Figure 2. Global Roundwood Production per Person, 1961–2008

Source: FAO, Census Bureau

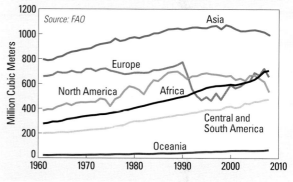

Figure 3. Roundwood Production by Region, 1961–2008

Source: FAO

whereby an organization such as the Forest Stewardship Council attests that wood sold to consumers was sustainably harvested. Certified forest area has grown steadily since the early 1990s, and in 2009 it reached 325 million hectares, about 8 percent of the world's forested area.[23] But contrary to the original intent of certification, which was to protect tropical forests, 80–90 percent of certified forest area is in nontropical countries in the northern hemisphere, and more than half is in North America.[24] Shares of national forest area that is certified range from 53 percent in Europe and 38 percent in North America to 5 percent in Oceania and 1 percent in Africa, Asia, and Latin America.[25]

How important certification will ultimately be depends in part on whether consumers in rapidly growing markets like China and India will demand sustainably produced wood products as rising incomes drive their greater consumption of wood and paper.[26]

FAO estimates that global demand for wood and fiber will double by 2030, but increasingly efficient use of roundwood suggests that production may increase by only 40 percent.[27] As a greater share of sawdust, wood chips, and other wood residues are reclaimed, and as paper recycling rates climb, the share of virgin industrial roundwood in total wood and fiber use is expected to fall from almost 70 percent in 2005 to about 50 percent in 2030.[28] Indeed, the greatest growth in industrial roundwood production is expected in the paper and paperboard sector, where recycling rates are likely to grow in the decades ahead.

Meanwhile, FAO estimates that fuelwood output will increase by 46 percent, from 2.6 billion cubic meters in 2005 to 3.8 billion cubic meters in 2030.[29] But the actual figure could be lower if a growing share of bioenergy comes from agricultural residues and energy crops rather than from forests. On the other hand, increases in the production of cellulosic biofuels, some of which may use wood-based feedstocks, could increase the use of roundwood-derived products.[30] Other factors that will shape the future use of roundwood products include the overall growth in population and economies, the share of global growth that is realized in developing countries (where use of roundwood products per person is likely to grow the fastest), and environmental policies and regulations that could ban logging in more forest area.[31]

Finally, the share of roundwood produced from planted area is projected to continue upward, with the global area reaching nearly 350 million hectares by 2030.[32] And one certifying agency estimates that 45 percent of the world's roundwood production could come from certified forests by 2017.[33]

Population and Society Trends

Satellite image by GeoEye

São Paulo, Brazil, with over 18 million people, is the largest urban area in the southern hemisphere.

For additional population and society trends, go to vitalsigns.worldwatch.org.

World Population Growth Slows Modestly, Still on Track for 7 Billion in Late 2011

Robert Engelman

---World population passed 6.9 billion in mid-2010, according to United Nations demographers, and is on track to reach 7 billion in late 2011.[1] (See Figure 1.) The number of people added to the population each year—79.3 million—has been consistent for nearly a decade. Since the world population is larger each year, of course, this consistent increment equates to a slow fall in the annual growth rate. From mid-2009 to mid-2010, the population grew 1.16 percent, compared with 1.32 percent annually a decade earlier and with slightly more than 2 percent four decades ago. (See Figure 2.)

At the same time, humanity's median age is consistently rising, a byproduct of longer life expectancy and the fact that women are having fewer children on average than their mothers had. (See Figure 3.) In 1970, the world's median age—the precise age at which half of all people are younger and half are older—was 22.1 years. In 2010, it is 29.1 years. Yet overall "youthening" was the consistent trend from 1950, when the median age was 24 years, until 1970. Since then the median age has risen by two to three

months every year, a trend that now shows no signs of slowing.

The overall growth and aging of human population mask an unprecedented range of demographic diversity. (See Table 1.) Many industrial countries are now experiencing either relatively slow population growth or—in Japan, Germany, and 14 East European countries—absolute decline. The combination of rising life expectancy and falling fertility has led these countries to experience significant population aging, meaning a rise in the median age. In contrast, many developing countries continue to grow rapidly and have still-large proportions of young people. Median ages are nonetheless rising slowly (albeit from low bases) in most of these countries for the same reasons as in industrial nations: increasing life expectancy and declining fertility. Some developing countries already have relatively low fertility accompanied by fairly rapid aging, with China being the most often discussed example.

Today 95 percent of population growth is occurring in the world's developing countries, already home to 82 percent of the world's people yet producing just 34 percent of gross world product in absolute dollar terms.[2] The largest family sizes and the most rapid population growth tend to occur in the least developed countries. Niger, Afghanistan, Uganda, Timor-Leste (East Timor), the Palestinian territories (West Bank and Gaza), Liberia, and Burkina Faso all have population growth rates above 3 percent a year, a rate that if maintained would see populations double in less than 25 years.

Regionally, most of the countries growing more rapidly than 2 percent a year are in sub-Saharan Africa (average growth rate, 2.4 percent), although a few are in Asia, home to 60 percent of all human beings. The latter conti-

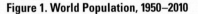

Figure 1. World Population, 1950–2010

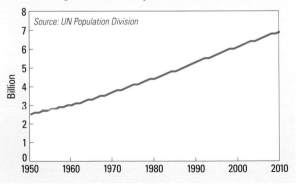

Source: UN Population Division

nent is especially demographically diverse. Its growth rates range from a high of 3.5 percent in Afghanistan to a negative one tenth of 1 percent in Japan. Among Asia's emerging economies, South Korea and Singapore are facing the prospect of population shrinkage in the near future, due primarily to very low fertility rates that could fail to replenish their populations over the next decade or two. Overall, the growth rate in Asia is just under 1.2 percent, almost identical to that of the world as a whole.

Latin America and the Caribbean together form the world's most demographically homogenous major region, with a 1.1 percent growth rate, just under the global average, and with few countries straying far from the average. Haiti is growing at 1.5 percent annually, while Honduras grows at nearly 2 percent. Uruguay has population dynamics similar to the industrial world, with a 0.3 percent growth rate. Relatively wealthy Chile is among the developing countries with a fertility rate below replacement, at 1.9 children per woman. Mexico, once among the world's more rapidly growing countries, now expands at just over 0.9 percent—essentially the same pace as the population of the United States. U.S. population growth, of course, includes net annual increases in immigrants, more of them from Mexico than from any other single country.

The industrial world also varies in its demographic dynamics, but around a narrow band of lower fertility and hence slower growth. Contrary to some perceptions, population growth continues among these wealthier countries as a whole, at almost exactly Uruguay's 0.3 percent annual rate, adding some 3.8 million people to the world each year. The English-speaking countries have higher growth rates, with Australia's population expanding at 1 percent annually while that of the United Kingdom grows at 0.5 percent. These numbers include net immigration, which in Australia and the United Kingdom, as in the United States, is a significant component of population growth. Population is declining in Germany (–0.1 percent), while in Eastern Europe the average growth rate is 0.04

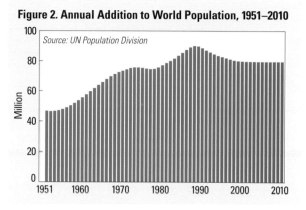

Figure 2. Annual Addition to World Population, 1951–2010

Source: UN Population Division

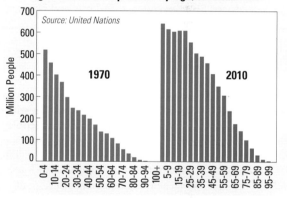

Figure 3. World Population by Age, 1970 and 2010

Source: United Nations

percent. According to national rather than U.N. data, Russia recently halted the shrinkage it had experienced since 1993 and may even have begun growing slowly again.[3]

One reason for Russia's loss of population up to now was a phenomenon that once was frequent among large human groups but is now much less familiar: declining life expectancy. Whether due to increasing alcoholism or stresses related to the large country's transition from its communist past, life expectancy at birth among both sexes fell from a peak above 69 years in the late 1960s to less than 65 in the early part of the present decade. Until life expectancy began rising in the past two or three years, Russia was among nine countries worldwide

Table 1. Regional Population Basics

Region	Population growth from 2009 to 2010 in numbers of people (and percent change)	Share of absolute global population, 2010	Share of the increase in global population from 2009 to 2010
		(percent)	(percent)
Africa	23,150,000 (2.29)	15	29
Asia	45,644,000 (1.1)	60	57
Europe	553,000 (0.08)	11	1
Latin America and the Caribbean	6,231,000 (1.07)	9	8
North America	3,299,000 (0.95)	5	4
Oceania	451,000 (1.27)	1	1

Source: U.N. Population Division, World Population Prospects: The 2008 Revision, Population Database, esa.un.org/unpp.

with falling life expectancies over most of the past two decades. These causes also characterize reduced life expectancy in Belarus and Ukraine. In six countries in Africa (the Democratic Republic of the Congo, Lesotho, South Africa, Swaziland, Zambia, and Zimbabwe), civil conflict and the high prevalence of HIV/AIDS have shortened lives.[4]

Some commentators contend that population growth may constrain future economic growth in high-fertility countries while population aging may do so in low-fertility ones.[5] Due in large part to population growth, demand is continuously rising for food, energy, commodities, and jobs, with the most rapid rates of population increase often in countries that are least economically productive at home and least able to afford imports. At the same time, in many industrial and some rapidly developing countries, labor forces are beginning to shrink proportionally and sometimes absolutely. This helps to improve wages—as in China in recent years—but it also raises questions about future support for the elderly and about competitiveness in a globalized economy. Many industrial and some developing countries have proportions of elderly unprecedented in demographic history, with 23 percent of Japan's current 127 million population being older than 64.

Overall, however, there is little agreement among economists and demographers about precisely how strongly these demographic forces

will shape future economic change. Recently, one group of demographers argued that population aging is exaggerated as a negative economic force, noting in particular that the "younger old" (people in their 60s and early 70s) are generally healthier than in previous generations and often are willing and able to work well beyond traditional retirement ages.[6]

Although many analysts assume that U.N. and other demographers predict world population to stabilize at roughly 9 billion by the middle of this century, this is not true. The U.N. Population Division's latest medium-fertility population projection (one of the three most often used projections, each of which is a conditional forecast based on different assumptions about future fertility rates) posits 9.15 billion people in 2050. But that number is projected not as a peak but simply a passing elevation sign. Population would still be growing by nearly 27 million annually at that time. Under the rarely cited low-fertility projection, world population would peak in the early 2040s at around 8 billion; under the high-fertility projection, it would hit nearly 10.5 billion in 2050 and still be rising rapidly. (Since the U.N. biennial population projection series does not go past 2050, there is no indication of when population will peak in the medium- and high-fertility projections, but the mid-century growth rates suggest no peak for either for many decades.) Taken together, these projections—all of which assume future fertility levels lower than today's—suggest the range of demographers' expectations. The actual demographic outcome hinges on population-related social policies—as well as on developments in health, the economy, and the environment—over the next four decades.

While most of the world's population continues to benefit from rising life expectancies, the future holds no promises that this trend will continue. The likelihood of climate change and the risks it poses to global food security, health, and security suggest at least one major potential challenge to falling mortality rates worldwide.

There is uncertainty as well about the future of fertility, which has declined dramatically worldwide since the early 1960s, when women gave birth to five children on average. Today the average is 2.53, almost half that number. More than any other demographic factor, falling fertility has slowed the rise of population from the 1960s to today. The fall of fertility is unpredictable, however. Within the population of industrial countries as a whole, fertility stopped falling at least by 2005 and has risen since

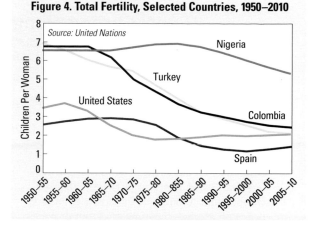

Figure 4. Total Fertility, Selected Countries, 1950–2010

then.[7] In many developing countries, meanwhile, fertility is falling relatively slowly and is still well above the so-called population replacement rate.[8] (See Figure 4.) These two trends suggest continued population growth for some time to come in both the industrial and the developing world.

Global Chronic Hunger Rises Above 1 Billion

Stephanie Pappas

In 2009, an estimated 1.02 billion people were classified as undernourished, 12 percent more than in 2008.[1] This means nearly one in six people on Earth suffers from undernourishment.[2] Undernourishment—or chronic hunger—is defined as regularly eating food that provides less than 1,800 kilocalories (kcal) a day.[3] In comparison, Americans, Canadians, and Europeans on average consume food that provides more than 3,400 kcal per day.[4]

Chronic hunger is only one aspect of malnutrition, a broad term for a multitude of conditions that hinder good health.[5] Malnutrition also includes overnutrition, which is eating more food than needed to meet energy requirements, and undernutrition, which is low levels of food intake or low absorption of food that is consumed. Generally, undernutrition applies to protein and fat deficiencies, but it is increasingly also being used to indicate a lack of essential vitamins and minerals. Three billion people suffer from chronic micronutrient deficiencies,

lacking adequate amounts of iron, iodine, and other important micronutrients in their diets.[6]

The 2009 Global Hunger Index (GHI) prepared by the International Food Policy Research Institute has fallen by one quarter since 1990.[7] The GHI analyzes several dimensions of hunger, including the proportion of undernourished in the population, the prevalence of undernourished children, and the rate of child mortality.[8] These data, however, are only tallied for 2002 to 2007 and do not include the impact of the recent food and economic crises.

Despite progress made during the 1980s and early 1990s, chronic hunger has been on the rise since the late 1990s. (See Figure 1.) In 29 countries a quarter or more of the population is affected by chronic hunger.[9] In Burundi, Comoros, the Democratic Republic of the Congo, and Eritrea, chronic hunger affects at least half of the population.[10] In line with the first Millennium Development Goal (MDG) established in 2000, the number of people suffering from chronic hunger and poverty was supposed to be halved by 2015.[11] The overall lack of progress, however, means that it is unlikely that MDG-1 will be reached.

The situation varies, of course, in different regions of the world. Latin America and the Caribbean is the only region that has been able to decrease the number of chronically hungry people.[12] The Asian and Pacific Islands region, although it has the largest population of hungry people, shows mixed results.[13] (See Figure 2.) South and Central Asia suffered setbacks, while Southeast Asia remains on track for meeting MDG-1.[14] The Near East and North Africa has been demonstrating slight though steady increases in hunger since 1990.[15] Due to rapid population growth, the overall number of hungry people in sub-Saharan Africa has increased,

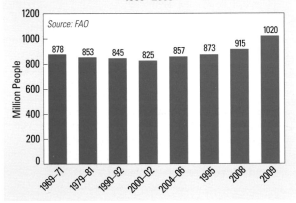

Figure 1. Number of Undernourished People in the World, 1969–2009

although the region did make strides in reducing the proportion of people suffering from chronic hunger.[16]

While poverty is almost always a factor, other causes of chronic hunger vary from region to region. In Asia, the low social and educational status of women contributes to high incidences of low birth weight and malnourished children under the age of five.[17] In the Near East and Latin America, political turmoil fuels food insecurity.[18] In sub-Saharan Africa, conflicts and high rates of HIV/AIDS hinder people's abilities to meet their calorie requirements.[19]

Investments in agriculture by governments, international lenders, and foundations are at a historic low. Only 4 percent of official development funds have been invested in agriculture over the last 15 years, and few donors have increased their commitments since 2000.[20] Public spending on agriculture is often lowest in countries with agriculture-based economies.[21] (See Figure 3.) In these countries the agricultural sector can generate approximately 29 percent of the gross domestic product (GDP) and employ 65 percent of the labor force.[22] Even in transforming and urbanized countries the industries and services linked by value chains to agriculture often account for more than 30 percent of the GDP.[23] Reduced agricultural investment increases a country's hunger problem by curtailing food production, limiting the ability to import food, and decreasing employment and income.[24]

Not surprisingly, the rural poor are most affected by hunger.[25] In countries such as Tajikistan and Eritrea, the lack of infrastructure inhibits the rural poor's ability to earn a living from farming by restricting their access to markets.[26] In other countries, such as Kenya and Ethiopia, increased farming on degraded land means that the rural poor are unable to grow enough food to eat or sell.[27]

While rural poverty remains higher in most countries, urban poverty is increasing at a faster rate.[28] In some cities, the urban poor have to pay five to seven times more, as a percentage of their income, than wealthier urban dwellers for

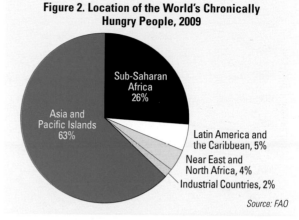

Figure 2. Location of the World's Chronically Hungry People, 2009

Sub-Saharan Africa 26%

Asia and Pacific Islands 63%

Latin America and the Caribbean, 5%

Near East and North Africa, 4%

Industrial Countries, 2%

Source: FAO

Figure 3. Agricultural Share of Gross Domestic Product and Public Agricultural Spending in Agricultural, Transforming, and Urbanized Countries, 2000

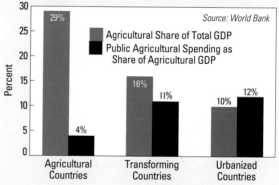

Source: World Bank

Agricultural Share of Total GDP
Public Agricultural Spending as Share of Agricultural GDP

Agricultural Countries: 29%, 4%
Transforming Countries: 16%, 11%
Urbanized Countries: 10%, 12%

access to clean water and sanitary food, further contributing to chronic hunger levels.[29]

Overall, women and children account for the highest proportion of the chronically hungry.[30] High food prices and lower incomes put poor households at an additional risk of not providing expectant mothers, infants, and children with adequate nutrition. For mothers, inadequate nutrition can result in low infant birth weight, poor health, and high instances of childbirth-related death.[31] For infants and children, even short-term malnutrition can result in permanent damage to health, brain activity, and

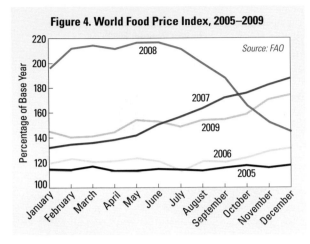

Figure 4. World Food Price Index, 2005–2009

Source: FAO

productivity.[32] More than one third of child deaths are related to inadequate nutrition.[33]

As a result of hunger and poor nutrition, people's productivity levels are lowered, pushing them further into poverty.[34] When more than 30 percent of the population is chronically undernourished, such as in Comoros, Kenya, and many other African countries, the growth of entire economies can be compromised.[35]

While world food prices have fallen from their 2008 spike, they remain well above pre-2007 levels, and the trend was steadily upward in 2009.[36] (See Figure 4.) The global economic recession has hit the world's poor hard, through decreasing real wages, unemployment, lower credit, shrinking remittances from abroad, and increasing pressures from urbanization.[37] The current recession has also caused cuts in both food aid and development funds, further threatening food security.[38]

Food aid programs have been affected by both the food price crisis of 2007 and the recession. Higher food prices in 2007 meant that these programs could not purchase as much food. Although prices began to drop in 2008, the recession has lessened the amount of money allocated for food aid. The U.S. Agency for International Development (USAID) reported that it was only able to donate $2.2 billion in 2009, a decrease of 15 percent from 2008.[39]

Climate change is also expected to add to the chronic hunger problem. Extreme weather events, such as droughts and floods, can decrease yields and cause both chronic and transitory food insecurity.[40] Chronic hunger is expected to increase across all developing countries, but it will especially affect the poorer rural communities in sub-Saharan Africa who rely on rain-fed agriculture as their main source of food.[41]

With issues such as climate change and decreased food aid threatening to raise the already high levels of chronic hunger, smallholder farms could potentially play a vital role in climate change mitigation and food security.[42] These farms can use agricultural practices that reduce carbon emissions, such as intercropping composting, and that at the same time stimulate farm productivity.[43] Climate change mitigation in and around farms can improve biodiversity and increase ecosystem services that improve farm capabilities.[44]

One way to address the problem of chronic hunger is to invest more in the agricultural sector and in developing sustainable agriculture programs.[45] In Haiti, prior to the earthquake in 2010 an estimated 46 percent of the population was undernourished.[46] Haiti relies on imports for 48 percent of its food, and food assistance meets 5 percent of national needs.[47] The destruction of the country's infrastructure during the earthquake made the delivery of imported food and food aid very difficult, and Haiti's underdeveloped agricultural sector is unable to supplement the shortage—placing more people at risk for chronic hunger. This tragedy demonstrates how critical a strong agricultural sector can be to a country.

The World Bank has increased its global lending for agriculture by 76 percent since 2006–08, with the largest share targeting agricultural development in Africa.[48] Other projects are promoting better farming practices, education, and access to markets to bolster the agricultural sector in sub-Saharan Africa. In Ethiopia, for example, the Dutch nongovernmental group Prolinnova is working with farmers to prevent soil erosion and is encouraging local innovations.[49] In

Tanzania, the World Vegetable Center is working with farmers to breed varieties of vegetables that do not need fertilizers and other chemicals.[50] In Zambia, USAID's PROFIT program is working to help link farmers to the private sector in order to increase incomes.[51]

Increasing the resources available to women could promote increased economic and agricultural productivity as well as better nutrition for families. In Eritrea, for example, the International Fund for Agricultural Development (IFAD) holds workshops where women learn how to make and market palm leaf fans and mats. These goods bring in additional income and provide the women with some financial independence.[52] In Pakistan, IFAD developed a microfinance program aimed at providing rural women with the capital necessary to start small businesses. In many cases, these women have become the main source of income for their families.[53]

Stephanie Pappas was an intern at Worldwatch Institute.

Educational Attainment Worldwide on the Rise

Kelsey Russell, Nausheen Khan, and Robert Engelman

People all over the world are completing more years of schooling than ever. More than 61 percent of individuals 15 or older—just over 3 billion people—finished at least some secondary school during their lifetimes as of 2010.[1] This proportion has risen from 36 percent in 1970 and from 50 percent in 1990.[2] (See Figure 1.) This category includes those who completed secondary school and those who went on to colleges and universities and perhaps graduated from there. Having advanced to secondary school or beyond not only indicates that individuals are better prepared for the future; it also highlights educational success, since students are unlikely to advance to higher educational levels without having completed prior schooling.

These educational attainment data are based on a novel assessment of the world's schooling compiled by the International Institute for Applied Systems Analysis (IIASA) in Austria and the Vienna Institute of Demography (VID).[3] (See Figure 2.) Unlike the World Bank and other school enrollment databases, which pro-vide static enrollment figures, the IIASA-VID approach estimates and measures total lifetime educational achievement—the highest level of schooling ever achieved by each person. This approach reveals changes in education levels reached by all adults rather than merely children and other people currently enrolled in school.

In 2010, according to the data, only about 1 in 10 adult males (adults here means everyone older than 15) and 1 in 5 adult females had no schooling whatsoever.[4] While their numbers have grown with world population generally, the proportion of unschooled or primary-schooled-only adults decreased from 64 percent of the adult population in 1970 to 39 percent today.[5] (See Figure 3.)

Increased levels of completed schooling are a key proxy indicator of improved human well-being. Education builds human capital, the personal resources people bring to economic and other aspects of human development.[6] Among women, education may improve their status and decisionmaking authority, and it correlates strongly with lower fertility and later childbearing, which slows population growth.[7]

Educated women are able to make better informed health choices for themselves and their children, and children of better-educated mothers have higher immunization and lower mortality rates.[8] For example, over roughly the past decade the proportions of child deaths before the age of five correlated almost perfectly with the educational attainment level of mothers in Kenya, Ethiopia, and Nigeria, according to recent U.S. health surveys.[9]

Finally, education is important for a nation's economic performance. Applying the IIASA-VID data (with detail by each five-year cohort in adult populations) to national economic outcomes, Wolfgang Lutz and colleagues found

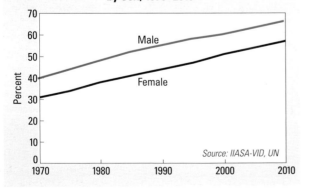

Figure 1. Share of World Population 15 and Older Who Have Completed Some Secondary or Higher Education, by Sex, 1970–2010

Male

Female

Source: IIASA-VID, UN

clear signals that having at least some secondary education or beyond "is a consistently significant determinant of a country's aggregate level of economic growth."[10]

Geographically, the highest average levels of completed education are found in North America and Europe, where 93 percent and 85 percent of adults respectively have completed at least some secondary school.[11] The lowest levels are found in Africa, where 38 percent of adults have completed at least some secondary education.[12] Latin America and the Caribbean and Asia represent a middle ground educationally, with 57 percent having completed some secondary education in both regions.[13]

A more significant divide than geography, however, may be development status. In 2010, using U.N. county categories, 89 percent of adults in more developed countries had attained some secondary education or higher, compared with 54 percent in less developed countries and 30 percent in the least developed countries.[14] In 2010, 36 percent of adults in the least developed countries had never attended school, while in the more developed countries only 1 percent fell into this category.[15]

Women's level of educational attainment in 2010 has improved significantly from 1970, when 41 percent of the female population had never been to school.[16] Today that proportion is less than half as large, with just 19 percent of women not having some schooling.[17] Not only are higher percentages of girls going to school than ever before, but more and higher proportions of young women are entering adulthood with some secondary or higher education. The number of women in 2010 who have attained some primary education is 620 million—25 percent —compared with 599 million men, or 24 percent, effectively closing a long-existing gender gap at this lowest level of schooling.[18]

However, men are still more likely than women to have completed some secondary or higher education; 66 percent of males fell into this category in 2010 compared with 40 percent in 1970, while 57 percent of women reached this level, up from 31 percent in 1970.[19] This

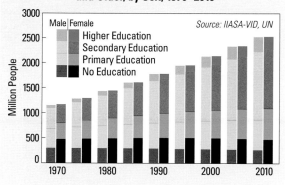

Figure 2. Educational Attainment, World Population 15 and Older, by Sex, 1970–2010

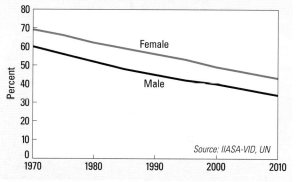

Figure 3. Share of World Population 15 and Older Who Have No Schooling or Have Completed Some Primary Education, by Sex, 1970–2010

indicates that the more important gender gap of achieving equality in secondary and higher educational attainment still persists and that the U.N. Millennium Development Goal of gender equity in primary and secondary education has not been achieved.[20]

This rise in women's education has its own intrinsic value, but it is also catalytic in social and human development generally. Not only is higher educational attainment among women likely to contribute powerfully to slower population growth through later childbearing and reduced fertility, it also appears to narrow social inequalities within countries.[21] Research has

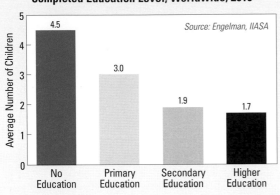

Figure 4. Average Number of Children per Woman by Completed Education Level, Worldwide, 2010

Source: Engelman, IIASA

found that the effect of individual women's education is statistically significant and more predictive of fertility than other factors such as income, rural-urban residence, or husband's education.[22]

Although achieving primary education in some of the least-developed countries may increase fertility due to improved nutrition and maternal health, as women's educational attainment rises beyond primary and into secondary school, the relationship between education and fertility changes from positive to negative.[23] According to data from IIASA, the average fertility of women who have received some secondary education is 1.9 children, fully 1.1 children below the average fertility level of women who

have received only primary education.[24] (See Figure 4.) Fertility falls even further, though not as dramatically, among women with some college or university education—to an average of 1.7 children per woman.[25] Other statistics indicate that seven years of educational attainment is the threshold for a fertility decline of 20 percent or more.[26]

As women become more educated, their literacy skills improve and they are better equipped to obtain and interpret information, including how to exercise their reproductive rights through the effective use of family planning.[27] Educated women have higher use of contraception and effective methods for timing childbearing or limiting family size than uneducated women do.[28] Women's autonomy—whether economic, physical, or emotional—is also a key factor in the fertility declines associated with higher levels of education.[29] And education levels correlate with lowered desired family sizes and higher demand for family planning.[30] Especially through this mechanism, and possibly through others as well, humanity's progress in achieving higher levels of completed schooling is a positive trend not only for economic and other aspects of development but for environmental sustainability generally.

Robert Engelman is the Vice President for Programs at Worldwatch. Kelsey Russell and Nausheen Khan were interns at the Institute.

Mobile Phone and Internet Use Grows Robustly

Erik Assadourian and Vanessa Damelio

The use of mobile telephones and the Internet continues to grow worldwide, and the two technologies are increasingly becoming integrated through advances like Internet-ready "smart" phones. In 2009, mobile phone subscriptions hit the 4.6 billion mark, doubling in less than four years.[1] (See Figure 1.) Their use has increased worldwide at over 21 percent annually over the past five years, and subscriptions are projected to reach 5 billion in 2010.[2] Internet use also grew to new levels—averaging 15 percent growth a year over the past five years—to reach almost 1.7 billion total users worldwide in 2009, about twice the usage rate in 2003.[3] (See Figure 2.)

The global average of mobile phone subscriptions per 100 inhabitants is 67, nearly four times the figure in 2002 of 18 per 100.[4] But this masks a wide variation: there were more than 100 subscriptions per 100 inhabitants in industrial countries in 2009 but only 57 per 100 in developing countries.[5] (See Figure 3.)

Sixty countries had more mobile phone subscriptions per 100 inhabitants than actual inhabitants in 2008, which can happen when consumers have more than one phone subscription.[6] The United Arab Emirates leads the world in this category, with 209 subscriptions per 100 inhabitants.[7] Italy tops the list in Europe, with 152 per 100 inhabitants, and the United States is in the middle of the pack worldwide, with 87 subscriptions per 100 inhabitants.[8]

The ratio of mobile phones to land lines is growing rapidly, particularly in countries where the expensive infrastructure for land lines has not already been developed. In 1999 there were two land lines for every mobile phone subscription worldwide.[9] In 2002, this ratio was even, and by 2008 there were 3.2 mobile phone subscribers for every land line.[10] Many countries

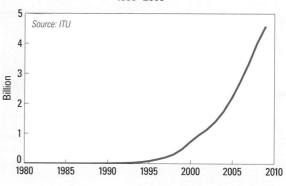

Figure 1. Mobile Phone Subscriptions Worldwide, 1980–2009

Source: ITU

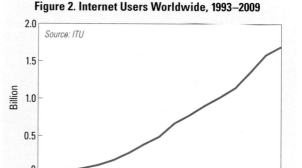

Figure 2. Internet Users Worldwide, 1993–2009

Source: ITU

that have leapfrogged past land lines have ratios much more heavily weighted toward mobile phone use. In Africa, for example, Sierra Leone has a ratio 10 times the world average, Kenya has a ratio 20 times larger, and Liberia has a ratio more than 100 times the world average.[11]

An estimated 26 percent of the world's population used the Internet in 2009.[12] This is nearly double the figure in 2003.[13] But again there is

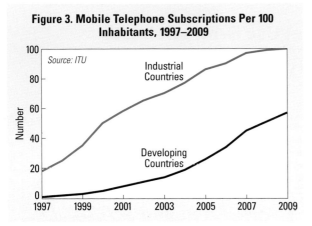

Figure 3. Mobile Telephone Subscriptions Per 100 Inhabitants, 1997–2009

wide variation in usage. In some industrial countries the majority of the population is online, with leading countries hitting 75–90 percent usage rates.[14] (See Figure 4.) Yet in 70 countries less than 10 percent of the population uses the Internet.[15]

Mobile phones that can get access to the Internet are one of the technologies expanding Internet usage. Globally, these smart phones accounted for 600 million of the total phones in circulation in 2009—a number projected to reach 1 billion by the end of 2010.[16] With smart phones driving an increase in mobile Internet access, there is also significant growth in advertising aimed at users through their mobile phones. In 2009, global mobile advertising reached $3.1 billion, and it is projected to grow by 45 percent a year, hitting $28.8 billion by 2014.[17]

Increased use of mobile phones and the Internet raises concerns about the environmental impact of obsolete devices. Electronic consumer products often contain toxic materials such as lead, cadmium, mercury, and flame retardants, all of which present serious health and environmental concerns.[18] In the United States, only 18 percent of computer products and 10 percent of mobile phones were recycled in 2007, and an estimated 2.3 million tons of e-waste entered landfills in 2005.[19] But this waste is also a potential source of valuable resources if recycled. One ton of mobile phones (about 6,000 phones) con-

tains $15,000 in precious metals.[20]

One recent positive development is the launch of the first global e-waste recycler certification program, which was announced by the Basel Action Network and endorsed by over 68 environmental organizations and corporations.[21] This program certifies environmentally and socially responsible recyclers so that electronics manufacturers and vendors can ensure that their products are recycled responsibly—including guarantees that no toxic waste will enter landfills or incinerators, compliance with global hazardous waste treaties, and significant worker safety protections.[22] Three U.S. recyclers had been fully certified as of April 2010 and another 50 are committed to being certified by September 2011.[23]

Internet and mobile phone usage has now become a large part of consumers' daily routine in many parts of the world, with the Internet being used regularly to shop, read news, and explore social networking sites like Facebook, which alone has over 400 million active users worldwide.[24] In 2008, Europeans on average spent 12 hours a week using the Internet, while Americans spent 13 hours a week.[25] Europeans also spent 143 minutes a month talking on their mobile phones in 2007, while Americans spent 798 minutes.[26] This in part reflects the relative cost of texting versus talking in these two markets. On average, Europeans text much more than Americans do, as minutes speaking on the phone tend to cost more in Europe. In the United Kingdom alone, people sent 97 billion text (SMS, for short message service) messages in 2009, up from 57 billion in 2007.[27]

Children, too, are increasingly wired. In 2009 in the United States, children between 8 and 18 years old spent on average one hour and 22 minutes on mobile phones and one hour and 29 minutes on a computer per day.[28]

Increasing numbers of people now suffer from Internet addiction, which recent psychological research finds correlates with depression.[29] In South Korea, the government has set up free treatment centers to combat Internet addiction.[30]

Mobile phones are also leading to new dangers as more people talk or text while driving. According to recent studies, talking on a mobile phone while driving can quadruple accident risk, and texting while driving can make accidents 23 times more likely.[31] Many state governments in the United States now ban texting and require drivers to use hands-free devices when talking on their phones. [32] These restrictions have so far not been successful in reducing accident rates, however. [33] Experts suggest that this is due to a continued level of cognitive distraction of drivers, which hands-free devices seem unable to reduce.[34] Other drivers may simply be disregarding the ban altogether. [35]

While new dangers have arisen with the growth of mobile phones and the Internet, these technologies are also creating new opportunities. Following the 2010 earthquake in Haiti, for instance, over 100,000 SMS messages were sent during disaster relief coordination, with many of them being translated and mapped; text messages also helped raise tens of millions of dollars of donations for relief efforts.[36] And in Congo, a British surgeon performed an amputation by following a colleague's instructions sent to him in text messages.[37]

SMS-based money transfers are also becoming a global phenomenon. In Kenya, for example, M-PESA (or mobile-pesa, which is the Kenyan currency) is a mobile phone application that allows its 9.7 million users to deposit, withdraw, and transfer money from their accounts.[38] A total of $5.3 billion was transferred between March 2007, when M-PESA began, and April 2010.[39] M-Kesho, introduced in Kenya in May 2010, gives mobile users without bank accounts access to financial services and modern banking by making micro-savings, micro-credit, and micro-insurance features available.[40]

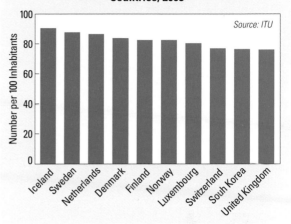

Figure 4. Internet Users per 100 Inhabitants, Top 10 Countries, 2008

Mobile phones are increasingly used to help monitor elections and coordinate political protests and revolutions. In Kenya's 2007 elections, an SMS code was used to report election-related violence, with comments and locations provided using Google Maps.[41] In Ukraine's Orange Revolution in 2004, mobile phones allowed demonstrators to coordinate protests against the rigged election, which led to a new one.[42] And despite efforts to restrict information following disputed elections in Moldova and Iran, the Internet and mobile phones were used to build international pressure for a democratic resolution.[43]

Erik Assadourian is a Worldwatch Senior Fellow and director of State of the World 2010: Transforming Cultures: From Consumerism to Sustainability. *Vanessa Damelio was a Transforming Cultures Project Assistant at Worldwatch.*

Notes

GLOBAL COAL USE STAGNATES DESPITE GROWING CHINESE AND INDIAN MARKETS (pages 12–15)

1. Totals based on BP, Statistical Review of World Energy 2010 (London: 2010).
2. International Energy Agency (IEA), *Coal Information 2010* (Paris: 2010); BP, op. cit. note 1.
3. BP, op. cit. note 1.
4. Ibid.
5. Calculated based on ibid.
6. Ibid.
7. Calculated based on IEA, op. cit. note 2, Section V, pp. 19–21.
8. Richard Morse and Gang He, *The World's Greatest Coal Arbitrage: China's Coal Import Behavior and Implications for the Global Coal Market*, Program on Energy and Sustainable Development, Working Paper #94 (Stanford, CA: Stanford University, August 2010).
9. BP, op. cit. note 1.
10. Ananth Chikkatur, *A Resource and Technology Assessment of Coal Utilization in India*, Pew Center on Global Climate Change (Arlington, VA: October 2008); Eric Yep, "Reliance Power Plans 100 Million Tons Per Year Coal Output," *Wall Street Journal*, 28 September 2010; IEA, op. cit. note 2, Section II, p. 14.
11. IEA, op. cit. note 2.
12. Ibid.
13. Calculations and Figure 4 from BP, op. cit. note 1.
14. BP, op. cit. note 1.
15. Ibid.
16. Ibid.
17. Calculated based on U.S. Energy Information Administration (EIA), "U.S. Coal Consumption by End-Use Sector," available at eia.gov/cneaf/coal/ quarterly/html/t32p01p1.html, viewed 4 October 2010.
18. Calculated based on EIA, "Net Generation by Energy Source: Total," *Electric Power Monthly with Data for June 2010*, 15 September 2010.
19. For example, see Xcel Energy, "Implementing Colorado's Clean Air–Clean Jobs Act," at www.xcelenergy.com.
20. Britt Burt and Shane Mullins, "U.S. Coal-Fired Power Development: Down but Not Out," *POWER Magazine*, October 2010.
21. U.S. Environmental Protection Agency, "EPA Issues Comprehensive Guidance to Protect Appalachian Communities from Harmful Environmental Impacts of Mountaintop Mining," press release (Washington, DC: 1 April 2010).
22. BP, op. cit. note 1; IEA, op. cit. note 2, Section II, p. 9.
23. IEA, op. cit. note 2.
24. Elizabeth Rosenthal, "As Europe Kicks Coal, Hungarian Town Suffers," *New York Times*, 15 September 2010.
25. BP, op. cit. note 1.
26. Ibid.; IEA, op. cit. note 2.
27. EIA, "Russia: Coal," at www.eia.doe.gov/emeu/cabs/Russia/Coal.html.
28. BP, op. cit. note 1.
29. Ibid.
30. Ibid.; IEA, op. cit. note 2, Section II, p. 3.
31. EIA, "Australia: Coal," at www.eia.doe.gov/emeu/cabs/Australia/Coal.html.
32. Calculated based on IEA, op. cit. note 2.
33. Program on Sustainable Energy and Development, Stanford University, "Global Coal Markets," at pesd.stanford.edu/research/coal_markets.

34. BP, op. cit. note 1.
35. Ibid.
36. Ibid.
37. Ibid.
38. Chris. J. H. Hartnady, "South Africa's Falling Coal Reserves," *South African Journal of Science*, September/October 2010.
39. EIA, "Australia: Electricity," at www.eia.doe.gov/emeu/cabs/South_Africa/Electricity.html; "World Bank Approves Loan for Coal-fired Power Plant in South Africa," *Washington Post*, 9 April 2010.
40. Calculations and Figure 3 based on BP, op. cit. note 1.
41. IEA, op. cit. note 2.

GROWTH OF BIOFUEL PRODUCTION SLOWS
(pages 16–18)

1. REN21, Renewables 2010 Global Status Report (Paris: 2010), p. 24.
2. Ibid.
3. BP, *BP Statistical Review of World Energy* (London: June 2010), p. 8; REN21, op. cit. note 1, p. 24.
4. REN21, op. cit. note 1.
5. Ibid.
6. Ibid., p. 56.
7. Ibid.; Renewable Fuels Association (RFA), *Climate of Opportunity: 2010 Ethanol Industry Outlook* (Washington, DC: 2010), p. 3
8. RFA, op. cit. note 7, p. 13.
9. REN21, op. cit. note 1.
10. Ibid.
11. Brazilian Sugarcane Industry Association (UNICA), "News," at The Industry- Background, at english.unica.com.br/content/show.asp?cntCode=D0B9E7BA-04AB-4637-9B69-7B2FECB82647.
12. REN21, op. cit. note 1.
13. Ibid., p. 25.
14. Ibid.
15. Ibid., p. 56.
16. Ibid.
17. U.S. Environmental Protection Agency (EPA), "EPA Lifecycle Analysis of Greenhouse Gas Emissions from Renewable Fuels," at www.epa.gov/otaq/renewablefuels/420f10006.htm.
18. EPA, "EPA Finalizes Regulations for the National Renewable Fuel Standard Program for 2010 and Beyond," at www.epa.gov/otaq/renewablefuels/420f10007.htm.
19. EPA, "EPA Grants E15 Waiver for Newer Vehicles/ A New Label for E15 is Being Proposed to Help Ensure Consumers Use the Correct Fuel," at yosemite.epa.gov/opa/admpress.nsf/0/BF822DDBEC29C0DC852577BB005BAC0F.
20. Matthew L. Wald, "A Bit More Ethanol in the Gas Tank," *New York Times*, 13 October 2010.
21. EPA, op. cit. note 17.
22. Council of the European Union, "Press Release, 2782nd Council Meeting, Transport, Telecommunications, and Energy, Brussels, 15 February 2007," press release (Brussels: 15 February 2007).
23. Oliver Interwildi and David King, "Quo Vadis Biofuels," *Energy and Environmental Science*, 2009: 2, pp. 343–46; International Energy Agency (IEA), *Sustainable Production of Second-Generation Biofuels* (Paris: 2010), pp. 22–23.
24. IEA, op. cit. note 23, p. 23; William T. Coyle, *Next-Generation Biofuels: Near-term Challenges and Implications for Agriculture* (Washington, DC: U.S. Department of Agriculture (USDA), Economic Research Service (ERS), 2010), p. 8.
25. IEA, op. cit. note 23.
26. David Tilman et al., "Carbon-Negative Biofuels from Low-Input High-Diversity Grassland Biomass," *Science*, 8 December 2006, pp. 1598–1600.
27. Matt Sanderson and Paul Adler, "Perennial Forages as Second Generation Bioenergy Crops," *International Journal of Molecular Sciences*, 20 May 2008, pp. 768–88.
28. Paul Adler et al., "Life-Cycle Assessment of Net Greenhouse-Gas Flux for Bioenergy Cropping Systems," *Ecological Applications*, vol. 17 (2007), pp. 675–91; Jorn Scharlemann and William Laurance, "How Green are Biofuels?" *Science*, 4 January 2008, pp. 43–44; Tilman et al., op. cit. note 26.
29. Tilman et al., op. cit. note 26; Adler et al., op. cit. note 28.
30. Angelo Gurgel, John M. Reilly, and Sergey Paltsev, *Potential Land Use Implications of a Global Biofuels Industry*, MIT Joint Program on the Science and Policy of Global Change, Report No. 155, (Cambridge, MA: March 2008); Martin Basne et al., "The Impact of First and Section Generation Biofuels on Global Agricultural Production, Trade, and Land Use," submitted for 11th Global Trade Analysis Project Conference, June 2008, at www.gtap.agecon.purdue.edu/resources/download/3693.pdf.
31. See, for example, Hong Yang et al., "Land and Water Requirements of Biofuel and Implications for Food Supply and the Environment in China,"

Energy Policy, May 2009, pp. 1876–85; Deepak Rajagopal, "Implications of India's Biofuel Policies for Food, Water, and the Poor," *Water Policy*, 3 January 2008, p. 1–12.

32. Coyle, op. cit. note 24.

33. Ibid.

34. Ibid.

35. Ibid.

36. USDA, ERS, "2008 Farm Bill Side-by-Side, Title IX: Energy," updated 20 August 2008 at www.ers.usda .gov/FarmBill/2008/Titles/TitleIXEnergy.htm.

37. IEA, op. cit. note 23; Dina Bacovsky, Michal Dallos, and Manfred Wörgetter, *Status of 2nd Generation Biofuels Demonstration Facilities in June 2010*, Report to IEA Energy Task 39 (Paris: 2010).

38. Gurgel, Reilly, and Paltsev, op. cit. note 30.

39. Bacovsky, Dallos, and Wörgetter, op. cit. note 37; Coyle, op. cit. note 24.

40. "Advanced Biofuels Tracking Database 1.1," *Biofuels-Digest*, updated 4 March 2010; Coyle, op. cit. note 24; Dynamic Fuels, at dynamicfuelsllc.com; Range Fuels, "Our First Commercial Plant," at www.range fuels.com/our-first-commercial-plant.html; BioMCN, "BioMCN Opens Largest 2nd Generation Biofuel Plant," press release (Delfzijl, Netherlands: 25 June 2010).

41. "Advanced Biofuels Tracking Database 1.1," op. cit. note 40.

42. "Fueled Again, Seaweed," *Biomass Energy Journal*, 22 June 2010.

43. "With a Little Kelp from My Friends: Macroalgae Projects, Concepts, Bloom," *Biofuels Digest*, 23 June 2010.

44. Ibid.

45. "Biofuels and Renewables Weekly," *Reuters*, 15 September 2010; "UK Biofuels 'Falling Short' on Environmental Standards," *BBC News*, 31 August 2010; Friends of the Earth International, "World Bank Land Grab Report Comment: Biofuels Cause Land Grabs," press release (Amsterdam: 8 September 2010).

46. Hart's Global Biofuels Center, as cited in "Global Biofuels Growth to Double by 2015," *PR Newswire*, 30 September 2009; IEA Medium-Term Oil and Gas Markets 2010, as cited in "IEA Raises 2009-2014 Global Biofuels Production Forecast," *Agra-net.com*, 28 June 2010.

NATURAL GAS USE FALLS BUT RENAISSANCE IS IN THE PIPELINE (pages 19–22)

1. All volumetric figures converted to cubic feet using the following conversion factors: 35.3 cubic feet = 1 cubic meter, 39.2 billion cubic feet = 1 million tons oil equivalent. BP, *Statistical Review of World Energy June 2010*, at www.bp.com/liveassets/bp_internet/ globalbp/globalbp_uk_english/reports_and_publ ications/statistical_energy_review_2008/STAGING/ local_assets/2010_downloads/statistical_review_of_ world_energy_full_report_2010.pdf, viewed 7 July 2010.

2. BP, op. cit. note 1.

3. Worldwatch calculation based on BP, op. cit. note 1.

4. BP, op. cit. note 1.

5. Supply for 150 years calculated based on 2009 consumption rate of 103.8 tcf; see note 1; 16,200 tcf is the mean of a 12,400 to 20,800 tcf range, with the low and high ends representing 10 and 90 percent probabilities, respectively. The estimate includes no unconventional resources outside the United States and Canada, as reliable assessments are not yet available. Top-down assessments suggest that around 6,000 tcf of recoverable unconventional gas resources could exist worldwide. Massachusetts Institute of Technology Energy Initiative (MITEI), *The Future of Natural Gas: Interim Report* (Cambridge, MA: MIT, 2010), p. 7.

6. Although natural gas prices are determined by long-term contracts in many regions, the United States has a strong spot market, the Henry Hub, and equivalents are emerging in Europe. While regional markets have historically been somewhat isolated from each other, with major price differentials, an increase in liquefaction capacity, growth in unconventional gas development, and a trend away from long-term contracts are making global markets more integrated and liquid. The U.S. Henry Hub spot price fell from an average of $8.85 per million Btu in 2008 to $3.89 in 2009—a drop of 56 percent. BP, op. cit. note 1.

7. BP, op. cit. note 1.

8. Ibid.

9. Worldwatch calculation based on U.S. Department of Energy (DOE), Energy Information Administration (EIA), *Annual Energy Outlook 2009* (Washington, DC: March 2009); on DOE, EIA, *Annual Energy Outlook 2010 Early Release Overview*, 14 December 2009, at www.eia.doe.gov/oiaf/aeo/index.html,

viewed 24 February 2010; and on DOE, EIA, Natural Gas Navigator, "Coalbed Methane Production," at tonto.eia.doe.gov/dnav/ng/ng_prod_coalbed_s1_a.htm, and "Shale Gas Production," at tonto.eia.doe.gov/dnav/ng/ng_prod_shalegas_s1_a.htm, both viewed 24 February 2010.

10. Colorado School of Mines, "Potential Gas Committee Reports Unprecedented Increase in Magnitude of U.S. Natural Gas Resource Base," press release (Golden, CO: 18 June 2009).

11. BP, op. cit. note 1.

12. Ibid.

13. DOE, EIA, *Natural Gas Year-In-Review 2009*, July 2010, at www.eia.gov/pub/oil_gas/natural_gas/feature_articles/2010/ngyir2009/ngyir2009.html?src=email#production, viewed 20 July 2010.

14. BP, op. cit. note 1.

15. Details on E.ON and Eni contracts from Judy Dempsey, "European Energy Giants Seek Lower Prices from Gazprom," *New York Times*, 24 February 2010. Gazprom's market share in Europe and Eurasia calculated based on 178.48 billion cubic meters of gas exported by Russia to Europe and Eurasia and 668.90 billion cubic meters of total consumption in Europe and Eurasia, excluding Russia, during 2009. BP, op. cit. note 1.

16. Jonathan Stern, "Continental European Long-Term Gas Contracts: Is a Transition away from Oil Product-Linked Pricing Inevitable and Imminent?" Oxford Institute for Energy Studies (Oxford, U.K.: September 2009).

17. International Energy Agency (IEA), *World Energy Outlook 2009* (Paris: 2009), pp. 460–62.

18. Vello Kuuskra and Scott Stevens, "Worldwide Gas Shales and Unconventional Gas: A Status Report" (Washington, DC: Advanced Resources International, December 2009); Marcin Sobczyk, "U.S. Giants Bet on Shale Gas in Poland," *Wall Street Journal* blog, 8 April 2010; Maciej Martewicz, "PGNiG Starts First Polish Shale Gas Well, Seeking to Cut Russia Dependence," *Bloomberg*, 9 July 2010.

19. The most famous of these projects is Nabucco, which together with the Italy-Greece-Turkey Interconnector, the Trans-Adriatic Pipeline, and White Stream comprises the Southern Corridor. Vladimir Socor, "Interest Surging in Azerbaijani Gas," *Eurasia Daily Monitor*, vol. 7, issue 128.

20. Alexandros Petersen, "Did China Just Win the Caspian Gas War?" *Foreign Policy*, July 2010.

21. BP, op. cit. note 1.

22. IEA, op. cit note 17, p. 366.

23. BP, op. cit. note 1.

24. "Delhi to Convert Coal Plants to Natural Gas," *ClimateWire*, 22 January 2010.

25. BP, op. cit. note 1.

26. Calculated based on BP, op. cit. note 1.

27. Figure of 14 percent calculated based on consumption data in BP, op. cit. note 1.

28. Petersen, op. cit. note 20.

29. BP, op. cit. note 1.

30. Ibid.; IEA, op. cit note 17, p. 485; Malcolm Brinded, Executive Director, Upstream International, "Natural Gas: Changing the Middle East Energy Landscape," speech delivered at the Middle East Petroleum and Gas Conference, Kuwait, 26 April 2010.

31. Brinded, op. cit. note 30.

32. IEA, op. cit note 17, p. 485.

33. BP, op. cit. note 1.

34. Ibid.

35. IEA, op. cit note 17, p. 498.

36. BP, op. cit. note 1.

37. Ibid.

38. IEA, op. cit note 17, p. 440.

39. Liquefaction capacity is based on a 2009 IEA projection of 313 billion cubic meters/year (11 trillion cubic feet/year); IEA, op. cit note 17, p. 440. Utilization calculated based on liquefaction capacity and 2009 LNG exports from BP, op. cit. note 1.

40. Share of primary fossil energy consumption calculated based on BP, op. cit. note 1. Carbon dioxide emissions include consumption and flaring, DOE, EIA, "Total Carbon Dioxide Emissions from the Consumption of Energy (Million Metric Tons), available at www.eia.gov/cfapps/ipdbproject/IEDIndex3.cfm?tid=90&pid=44&aid=8, viewed 20 July 2010.

41. See, for example, Christopher Flavin and Saya Kitasei, *The Role of Natural Gas in a Low-Carbon Energy Economy* (Washington, DC: Worldwatch Institute, April 2010).

42. See, for example, the IEA's 450 Scenario and the MITEI model. IEA, op. cit. note 17; MITEI, op. cit. note 5.

WORLD NUCLEAR GENERATION STAGNATES (pages 23–25)

1. International Atomic Energy Agency (IAEA), *Nuclear Power Reactors in the World* (Vienna: 2009), Table 7.

2. IAEA, "International Atomic Energy Agency Power Reactor Information System (IAEA-PRIS)," online database, at www.iaea.org/programmes/a2.

3. Ibid.

4. IAEA, op. cit. note 1.

5. Mycle Schneider et al., *World Nuclear Industry Status Report 2009* (Paris: German Federal Ministry of Environment, Nature Conservation and Reactor Safety, 2009), Annex 2.

6. Number of decommissioned plants is the 2008 stat from Schneider et al., op, cit. note 5, added to the three reactors decommissioned in 2009, from IAEA-PRIS.

7. Schneider et al., op. cit. note 5 p. 5.

8. World Nuclear Association, "Nuclear Power in Japan," factsheet, at www.world-nuclear.org/info/inf79.html.

9. Ibid.

10. Steven Chu, "Conference Call on Loan Guarantee for Nuclear Plant in Georgia," *Teleconference*, 16 Feb 2010.

11. Lazard, *Levelized Cost of Energy Analysis – Version 3.0* (2009), p. 10.

12. Steven Mufson, "Nuclear Power Projects Face Financial Hurdles, *Washington Post*, 2 March 2010.

13. Chu, op. cit. note 10.

14. IAEA, op. cit. note 2.

15. Ibid.

16. Schneider et al., op. cit. note 5, p. 15.

17. IAEA, op. cit. note 2.

18. Ibid.

19. Saeromi Shin, "Korea Electric, Doosan Jump on U.A.E. Nuclear Order," *Bloomberg News*, 28 December 2009.

20. BP, *Statistical Review of World Energy June 2009*, online database, at www.bp.com/multipleimagesection.do?categoryId=9023755&contentId=7044552.

21. Schneider et al., op. cit. note 5, p. 5; "World Net Nuclear Electric Power Generation (Billion Kilowatthours), 1980–2006" and "World Total Net Electricity Generation (Billion Kilowatthours), 1980–2006," from Energy Information Administration, U.S. Department of Energy, *International Energy Annual 2006*, at www.eia.doe.gov/iea/elec.html.

22. Schneider et al., op. cit. note 5, p. 5.

23. Ibid.

24. Ibid.

25. Ibid., p. 6.

WIND POWER GROWTH CONTINUES TO BREAK RECORDS DESPITE RECESSION (pages 26–28)

1. Global Wind Energy Council (GWEC), "Global Installed Wind Power Capacity 2008/2009 (MW)," at www.gwec.net/fileadmin/documents/PressReleases/PR_2010/GWEC%20forecast%20-%20annex.pdf, viewed 21 April 2010. Note that additions and total capacity account for decommissioning of 134.3 megawatts of capacity. The latest figures for 2009 wind power capacity installations released by GWEC differ slightly from those released by the World Wind Energy Association (WWEA), *World Wind Energy Report 2009* (Bonn: March 2010). For example, WWEA reports total added capacity in 2009 to be 38,312 megawatts, whereas GWEC reports total added wind capacity to be 38,343 megawatts. More significant differences exist for some individual countries: WWEA reports China's cumulative installed wind capacity at the end of 2009 to be 26,010 megawatts, whereas GWEC reports this figure to be 25,805 megawatts. GWEC's numbers for 2009 global and national wind statistics outside of North America and Europe are used for consistency throughout this article.

2. Ibid.

3. WWEA, op. cit. note 1.

4. GWEC, op. cit. note 1.

5. WWEA, op. cit. note 1.

6. Ibid. GWEC estimates new Chinese wind additions at 13,800 megawatts; GWEC, op. cit. note 1. BTM Consult estimates new Chinese wind additions at 13,750 megawatts; BTM Consult, "World Market Update 2009 (Forecast 2010-2014)," press release (Ringkøbing, Denmark: 29 March 2010).

7. WWEA, op. cit. note 1, p. 12; Jeremy van Loon, "Renewable Energy Investment May Reach $200 Billion in 2010," *Bloomberg*, 17 March 2010.

8. Xina Xie and Michael Economides, "Great Leap Forward for China's Wind Energy," *Energy Tribune*, 30 July 2009.

9. GWEC, op. cit. note 1.

10. BTM Consult, op. cit. note 6.

11. GWEC, op. cit. note 1.

12. American Wind Energy Association (AWEA), *AWEA Year End 2009 Market Report* (Washington, DC: January 2010).

13. U.S. Department of Energy, Energy Information Administration, *Electric Power Monthly with Data for December 2009*, 15 March 2010, "Table ES3: New

and Planned U.S. Electric Generating Units by Operating Company, Plant and Month."

14. Jad Mouawad, "Wind Power Grows 39% for the Year," *New York Times*, 26 January 2010.

15. GWEC., op. cit. note 1.

16. AWEA, op. cit. note 12.

17. Ibid.

18. Ibid.

19. European Wind Energy Association (EWEA), *Wind in Power: 2009 European Statistics* (Brussels: February 2010).

20. Ibid.

21. Ibid.

22. Ibid.

23. GWEC, "Spain," at www.gwec.net/index.php?id=131, viewed 30 March 2010.

24. "Wind Energy Has Consolidated as the Third Technology of the Power System," *Eolic Energy News* (Spanish Wind Energy Association), 12 January 2010.

25. Ibid.

26. Ibid.; GWEC, op. cit. note 1.

27. EWEA, op. cit. note 19.

28. Ibid.

29. WWEA, op. cit. note 1.

30. Ibid.

31. Ibid.

32. GWEC., op. cit. note 1.

33. Ibid.

34. Ibid.

35. BTM Consult, op. cit. note 6.

36. EWEA, *The European Offshore Wind Industry—Key Trends and Statistics 2009* (Brussels: January 2010).

37. Ibid.

38. Ibid., p. 6.

39. WWEA, op. cit. note 1, p. 7.

40. "China Speeds Up Offshore Wind Power Construction," *People's Daily Online*, 20 March 2010.

41. GWEC, "Global Wind Power Boom Continues Despite Economic Woes," press release (Brussels: 2 March 2010).

42. Figure for 2009 from WWEA, op. cit. note 1; figure for 2008 from GWEC, "Climate Change and Energy Security Drive Global Wind Power Boom: US & China Market Break All Previous Records," press release (Brussels: 2 February 2009).

43. WWEA, op. cit. note 1.

44. BTM Consult, op. cit. note 6.

RECORD GROWTH IN PHOTOVOLTAIC CAPACITY AND MOMENTUM BUILDS FOR CONCENTRATING SOLAR POWER (pages 29–31)

1. "Photovoltaics in 2009 – All Up and Germany Soars," *Bloomberg New Energy Finance*, 13–19 April 2010.

2. Ibid.; National Renewable Energy Laboratory (NREL), *2008 Solar Technologies Market Report* (Golden, CO: 2010); Worldwatch estimate also based on system production in Stuttgart, Germany, estimated using NREL, PVWatts (version 1), at rredc.nrel.gov/solar/calculators/PVWATTS/version1/International/pvwattsv1_intl.cgi, and on European household electricity consumption of 3.9 megawatt-hours per year derived from Eurostat, European Commission, at epp.eurostat.ec.europa.eu/portal/page/portal/statistics/search_database.

3. NREL, "Concentrating Solar Power Projects with Operational Plants," at www.nrel.gov/csp/solarpaces/; Solar Energy Industries Association (SEIA), *US Solar Industry Year in Review 2009* (Washington, DC: 2010).

4. Percent in Germany from Federal Ministry for the Environment, Nature Conservation and Nuclear Safety, *Development of Renewable Energy Sources in Germany 2009* (Berlin: March 2010), p. 8; percent in Spain is Worldwatch calculation based on Comisión Nacional de Energía (CNE), "Régimen Especial de Produccioón de Energía Eléctrica en España," workbook, 10 March 2010 (Spanish) and on Pedro Rivero Torre, "Balance Energético 2009 y Perspectivas 2010," Asociación Española de la Industria Eléctrica, 19 April 2010.

5. "Photovoltaics in 2009," op. cit. note 1; European Photovoltaic Industry Association (EPIA), "A Bright Sun Shines on the Solar Photovoltaic Electricity Market," press release (Brussels: 12 April 2010); Federal Network Agency, "Installed Capacity of Solar Systems in 2009 Increased by over 60 Percent," press release (Bonn: 9 April 2010).

6. Federal Network Agency, op. cit. note 5.

7. "Photovoltaics in 2009," op. cit. note 1.

8 NREL, *2008 Solar Technologies Market Report*, op. cit. note 2; EPIA, op. cit. note 5.

9. Alasdair Cameron, "Spanish PV after the Crash," *RenewableEnergyWorld.com*, 29 April 2010.

10. "Photovoltaics in 2009," op. cit. note 1.

11. EPIA, op. cit. note 5; Osamu Onodera, "Renewable Energy Policies for Development and Deployment,"

presentation, Ministry of Economy, Trade and Industry, Japan, March 2010.

12. SEIA, op. cit. note 3.

13. Ibid.; CNE, op. cit. note 4

14. NREL, op. cit. note 3; SEIA, op. cit. note 3.

15. NREL, op. cit. note 3; SEIA, op. cit. note 3.

16. "Localización de Centrales Termosolares en España," Protermo Solar, *Boletín de Noticias*, April 2010.

17. David Appleyard, "Parabolic Growth, CSP Moves into the Mainstream," *RenewableEnergyWorld.com*, 9 April 2010.

18. NREL, op. cit. note 3.

19. "Martin Next Generation Solar Energy Center FAQs," Florida Power & Light Company, at www.fpl.com/environment/solar/martin_faq.shtml.

20. *PV News*, Prometheus Institute, and Greentech Media, "26th Annual Data Collection Results: Another Bumper Year for Manufacturing Masks Turmoil," May 2010.

21. Ibid.

22. First Solar, "First Solar Corporate Overview," 1 March 2010.

23. PV News, Prometheus Institute, and Greentech Media, op. cit. note 20.

24. Ibid.

25. "Selections for Section 48C Manufacturing Tax Credit," Office of the President, Washington, DC, at www.whitehouse.gov/sites/default/files/48c_selection_011310.xls.

26. Bolko von Roedern, "Best Production-Line PV Module Efficiency Values" (Golden, CO: NREL, 2010).

27. NREL, *2008 Solar Technologies Market Report*, op. cit. note 2.

28. "Thin-film's Share of Solar Panel Market to Double by 2013," *RenewableEnergyWorld.com*, 13 November 2009.

29. PV News, Prometheus Institute, and Greentech Media, op. cit. note 20.

30. Nominal prices from NREL, *2008 Solar Technologies Market Report*, op. cit. note 2, p. 60.

31. NREL, *2008 Solar Technologies Market Report*, op. cit. note 2; NREL, *The Effects of the Financial Crisis on Photovoltaics: An Analysis of Changes in Market Forecasts from 2008 to 2009* (Golden, CO: 2009).

32. "Solarbuzz Reports World Solar Photovoltaic Market Grew to 7.3 Gigawatt in 2009," *Solarbuzz.com*, 15 March 2010; NREL, op. cit. note 31.

33. NREL, *Feed-in Tariff Policy: Design, Implementation, and RPS Policy Interactions* (Golden, CO: 2009).

34. PV News, Prometheus Institute, and Greentech

Media, "Letter From the Editor," February 2010; Svetlana Kovalyova, "UPDATE 2—Italy New Solar Incentives Seen in April," *Reuters*, 25 March 2010; PV News, Prometheus Institute, and Greentech Media, "Czech Lawmakers Approve Curbs to Solar Boom," April 2010.

35. Miguel Mendonça and David Jacobs, "Feed in Tariffs Go Global: Policy in Practice," *RenewableEnergyWorld.com*, 18 September 2009.

36. United Kingdom from PV News, Prometheus Institute, and Greentech Media, "UK Unveils Feed-in-Tariff," February 2010; Greece from PV News, Prometheus Institute, and Greentech Media, "Greece Introduces New Incentives for Small Rooftop PV," February 2010; Ontario from PV News, Prometheus Institute, and Greentech Media, "Samsung Begins Green Push with Ontario Deal," February 2010.; Taiwan from PV News, Prometheus Institute, and Greentech Media, "Taiwan Sets Wholesale Rates for Renewable Energy: Unveils Asia's Biggest Solar Power Plant," January 2010.

37. International Energy Agency, *IEA PV Power Newsletter*, September 2009.

38. NREL, op. cit. note 33; North Carolina Solar Center, "DSIRE Solar – Summary Maps," at www.dsireusa.org/solar/summarymaps.

39. International Energy Agency, op. cit. note 37.

40. Onodera, op. cit. note 11.

41. Ministry of New and Renewable Energy, "Jawaharlal Nehru National Solar Mission, Towards Building SOLAR INDIA" and "Government Announces Jawaharlal Nehru National Solar Mission" (New Delhi: undated and 23 November 2009).

42. PV News, Prometheus Institute, and Greentech Media, "New Amendment in China to Boost Renewable Energy Purchases," January 2010; National Development and Reform Commission, *China's Policy's and Actions for Addressing Climate Change – The Progress Report 2009* (Beijing: November 2009); Zhang Qi, "China Hikes 2011 Solar Power Target," *China Daily*, 3 July 2009.

43. "Photovoltaics in 2009," op. cit. note 1; NREL, op. cit. note 3; SEIA, op. cit. note 3.

44. First Solar, "First Solar and Ordos Take Key Step Forward in 2GW China Project," press release (Beijing: 17 November 2009); eSolar, "eSolar Partners With Penglai on Landmark Solar Thermal Agreement For China," press release (Pasadena, CA: 8 January 2010).

AUTO INDUSTRY IN TURMOIL BUT CHINESE PRODUCTION SURGES (pages 32–34)

1. Colin Couchman, IHS Global Insight Automotive Group, London, e-mail to author, 13 January 2010.
2. Ibid.
3. Ibid.
4. Michael Renner, Vehicle Production Rises Sharply," *Vital Signs 2007–2008* (New York: W. W. Norton & Company, 2007), p. 66; Michael Renner, "Global Auto Industry in Crisis," *Vital Signs Online*, 21 May 2009.
5. Couchman, op. cit. note 1.
6. Ibid.
7. Ibid.
8. Ibid.
9. International Organization of Motor Vehicle Manufacturers, "2008 Production Statistics," at oica.net/category/production-statistics, viewed 8 January 2010.
10. Ibid.
11. Calculated on basis of data provided by Couchman, op. cit. note 1.
12. PricewaterhouseCoopers Automotive Institute (PWC), "Autofacts Light Vehicle Capacity Data," at www.pwcautomotiveinstitute.com/datapage.asp, viewed 5 January 2010.
13. Ibid.
14. Ibid.
15. PWC, "Autofacts Topline Data," at www.pwcautomotiveinstitute.com/data.asp, viewed 5 January 2010. PWC statistics refer to "alliance groups" in the sense that smaller (subsidiary or affiliated) companies are included in these totals.
16. Ibid.
17. Ibid.
18. Carlos Gomes, "On the Road to Recovery in 2010," *Global Auto Report*, 29 December 2009, p. 1.
19. Ibid.
20. Ibid.
21. Ibid., p. 2.
22. Ibid.
23. "Japan Car Sales Seen Up in 2010, 1st Rise in 6 Years," *Reuters*, 24 December 2009; Japan Automobile Manufacturers Association, "Japan's Motor Vehicle Statistics," at www.jama.org/statistics/motorvehicle/sales/mv_sales_year.htm, viewed 8 January 2010.
24. Matthew Dolan and Kate Linebaugh, "Toyota, Ford Show Year-End Sales Gain," *Wall Street Journal*, 6 January 2010.
25. Ibid.
26. Lester R. Brown, "U.S. Car Fleet Shrank by Four Million in 2009—After a Century of Growth, U.S. Fleet Entering Era of Decline," Earth Policy Institute, 6 January 2010, at www.earth-policy.org/index.php?/plan_b_updates/2010/update87.
27. Ibid.
28. Michael Renner, "How Do You Say 'Clunker' in French?" *Worldwatch Green Economy blog*, 18 August 2009, at blogs.worldwatch.org/greeneconomy/how-do-you-say-clunker-in-french.
29. Sharon Terlep, "Car Makers on Edge in Europe," *Wall Street Journal*, 13 January 2010.
30. Gomes, op. cit. note 18, p. 2.
31. Ibid.
32. Ibid.
33. Colin Couchman, IHS Global Insight Automotive Group, London, e-mail to author, 14 January 2010.
34. Ibid.
35. Ibid.
36. Kate Linebaugh, "Electrics, Hybrids Star at Auto Show," *Wall Street Journal*, 8 January 2010.
37. PWC, op. cit. note 15.
38. Ibid.
39. Ibid.
40. The Boston Consulting Group, *Batteries for Electric Cars: Challenges, Opportunities, and the Outlook to 2020* (Boston, MA: January 2010), p. 7.
41. "Reported US Hybrid Sales Up 42% in December, Down 7.5% for CY 2009; New Vehicle Market Share of 2.8% for CY 2009," Green Car Congress, 7 January 2010, at www.greencarcongress.com/2010/01/hybsales-20100107.html#more.
42. Ibid.
43. Toyota Becomes Japan's Best-selling Car in 2009," *Xinhua*, 8 January 2010.
44. Environment America, *Plug-in Cars: Powering America Toward a Cleaner Future* (Boston: January 2010).
45. U.S. National Academy of Sciences, "Plug-In Hybrid Vehicle Costs Likely to Remain High, Benefits Modest for Decades," press release (Washington, DC: 14 December 2009).
46. Ibid.
47. Ibid.

AIR TRAVEL TRENDS MIXED AS CARBON FOOTPRINT GROWS (pages 35–37)

1. International Civil Aviation Organization (ICAO), *Annual Report of the Council 2008* (Montreal: 2009);

ICAO Statistics Section, e-mail to Zoë Chafe, Worldwatch Institute, 20 January 2005. Figures for 1950–69 do not include states formerly within the Soviet Union.

2. ICAO, *Annual Report*, op. cit. note 1; ICAO Statistics Section, op. cit. note 1.

3. ICAO, *Annual Report*, op. cit. note 1; ICAO Statistics Section, op. cit. note 1.

4. ICAO, *Annual Report*, op. cit. note 1; ICAO Statistics Section, op. cit. note 1.

5. ICAO, *Annual Report*, op. cit. note 1; ICAO Statistics Section, op. cit. note 1.

6. ICAO, "Passenger Traffic to Rebound in 2010 After Disastrous 2009," press release (Montreal: 13 July 2010).

7. Ibid.

8. ICAO, *Annual Report*, op. cit. note 1; ICAO Statistics Section, op. cit. note 1; ICAO, "Marginal Traffic Growth and Fuel Hedging Losses Take Toll on Airline Industry in 2008," press release (Montreal: 5 June 2009).

9. ICAO, *Annual Report*, op. cit. note 1; ICAO Statistics Section, op. cit. note 1; ICAO, op. cit. note 8.

10. ICAO, *Annual Report*, op. cit. note 1; ICAO Statistics Section, op. cit. note 1; ICAO, op. cit. note 8.

11. ICAO, *Annual Report*, op. cit. note 1; ICAO Statistics Section, op. cit. note 1.

12. ICAO, op cit. note 8.

13. ICAO, op. cit. note 6.

14. Ibid.

15. Energy Information Administration, U.S. Department of Energy, "Weekly All Countries Spot Price FOB Weighted by Estimated Export Volume," at www.eia.doe.gov/dnav/pet/hist/LeafHandler.ashx?n=PET&s=WTOTWORLD&f=W, viewed 7 July 2010.

16. Government Accountability Office, "Aviation and Climate Change: Aircraft Emissions Expected to Grow, but Technological and Operational Improvements and Government Policies Can Help Control Emissions" (Washington, DC: 8 June 2009).

17. T. Damassa, *Carbon Dioxide (CO$_2$) Inventory Report for Calendar Year 2008* (Washington, DC: World Resources Institute, 2010).

18. Ibid.

19. Elisabeth Rosenthal, "Britain Curbing Airport Growth to Aid Climate," *New York Times,* 1 July 2010.

20. U.N. Framework Convention on Climate Change, *Report on National Greenhouse Gas Inventory Data for the Period 1990–2005* (Bonn: 2007).

21. K. Ribeiro et al., "Transport and Its Infrastructure," in Intergovernmental Panel on Climate Change, *Climate Change 2007: Mitigation. Contribution of Working Group III to the Fourth Assessment Report* (Cambridge, U.K.: Cambridge University Press, 2005).

22. Ibid.

23. Ibid.

24. European Union (EU), "Questions and Answers on Aviation and Climate Change," memo (Brussels: 20 December 2006).

25. Tom Young, "China Attacks EU Efforts to Tackle Aviation Emissions," *BusinessGreen,* 9 June 2010.

26. EU, op. cit. note 24.

27. Ibid.

28. Sustainable Aviation, *Progress Report 2009*, at www.sustainableaviation.co.uk/pages/default/key-documents.html, viewed 7 July 2010.

29. U.K. Department for Transport, "The Future of Air Transport—White Paper and the Civil Aviation Bill," Chapter 3.35, 16 December 2003, at webarchive.nationalarchives.gov.uk/+/http://www.dft.gov.uk/about/strategy/whitepapers/air/.

30. U.K. Department of Energy and Climate Change, "Climate Change Act 2008," March 2009.

31. Rosenthal, op. cit. note 19.

32. Jessica Shankleman, "Lufthansa Plans Low Carbon Alternative Fuel by 2012," *BusinessGreen*, 11 May 2010.

33. Ibid.

34. Green Car Congress, "British Airways Partnering with Solena on Renewable Jet Fuel Plant; F-T Biojet Use Targeted for 2014," at www.greencarcongress.com/2010/02/ba-solena-20100215.html, viewed 19 July 2010.

35. Ibid.; British Airways Press Office, "BA Fuels Green Revolution," at press.ba.com/?p=904, viewed 19 July 2010.

36. Jennifer Waters, "Higher Fares, Fees Rev Up Airlines," *Wall Street Journal,* 8 August 2010.

37. Ibid.

38. International Air Transport Association (IATA), "IATA Brings Transparency to Baggage Rules—New Simplifying the Business Project," press release (Montreal: 8 June 2010).

39. Ibid.

40. IATA, *Annual Report 2010* (Montreal: 2010).

WORLD WILL COMPLETELY MISS 2010 BIODIVERSITY TARGET (pages 40–42)

1. International Union for Conservation of Nature (IUCN), *The IUCN Red List of Threatened Species 2009.2,* "Summary Statistics," Table 1.
2. Ibid., Table 7.
3. Ibid., Table 1.
4. Jean-Cristophe Vié et al., "The IUCN Red List: A Key Conservation Tool," in Jean-Cristophe Vié, Craig Hilton-Taylor, and Simon N. Stuart, eds., *Wildlife in a Changing World: An Analysis of the 2008 IUCN Red List of Threatened Species* (Gland, Switzerland: IUCN, 2009), p. 4.
5. Ibid.
6. IUCN, op. cit. note 1, Table 1; "Preface," in Vié, Hilton-Taylor, and Stuart, op. cit. note 4, p. ix.
7. Vié et al., op. cit. note 4, p. 16.
8. IUCN, op. cit. note 1.
9. Craig Hilton-Taylor et al., "State of the World's Species," in Vié, Hilton-Taylor, and Stuart, op. cit. note 4, p. 16; IUCN Species Survival Commission, "Sturgeon More Critically Endangered than Any Other Group of Species," press release (Gland, Switzerland: 18 March 2010).
10. Hilton-Taylor et al., op. cit. note 9, p. 34.
11. Ibid., p. 35.
12. IUCN Species Survival Commission, "Modern Lifestyle Threatens Oldest Seed Plants on Earth," press release (Gland, Switzerland: 2 July 2003).
13. IUCN Species Survival Commission, op. cit. note 9.
14. Ibid.
15. Ibid.
16. Ibid.
17. Hilton-Taylor et al., op. cit. note 9, pp. 19–24.
18. Ibid., Figure 6.
19. Ibid., pp. 19–24.
20. Ibid.
21. Ibid.; IUCN, "Impact of Nature's Invading Aliens Measured for First Time," press release (Gland, Switzerland: 25 January 2010).
22. Hilton-Taylor et al., op. cit. note 9, pp. 19–24.
23. Ibid., pp. 28–32.
24. Ibid.
25. IUCN Species Survival Commission, "Case Studies of Threatened Species," 12 November 2008, at www.iucn.org/about/work/programmes/species/red_list/2008_threatened_species_photo_gallery___case_studies.
26. Hilton-Taylor et al., op. cit. note 9, pp.24–28.
27. BirdLife International, *State of the World's Birds: Indicators for Our Changing World* (Cambridge, U.K.: 2008), p. 5.
28. Ibid.
29. Ibid., p. 6.
30. North American Bird Conservation Initiative, U.S. Committee, *The State of the Birds, United States of America, 2009* (Washington, DC: 2009), p. 4.
31. Ibid., p. 18.
32. Ibid.
33. Ibid., p. 16.
34. National Oceanic and Atmospheric Administration, "Sea ice Cover," *Arctic Report Card: Update for 2009* (Washington, DC: October 2009).
35. North American Bird Conservation Initiative, op. cit. note 30, p. 16.
36. Intergovernmental Panel on Climate Change, *Climate Change 2007: The Physical Science Basis* (Cambridge, U.K.: Cambridge University Press, 2007), p. 403.
37. B. A. Polidoro, "Status of the World's Marine Species," in IUCN, *Wildlife in a Changing World: An Analysis of the 2008 IUCN Red List of Threatened Species* (Gland, Switzerland: 2009), pp. 60–61.
38. Ibid.
39. Ove Hoegh-Guldberg, "Climate Change, Coral Bleaching and the Future of the World's Coral Reefs," *Marine & Freshwater Research,* 1999, pp. 839–66.
40. IUCN Species Survival Commission, "Climate Change and Species," at www.iucn.org/about/work/programmes/species/our_work/climate_change_and_species.
41. IUCN, "Species Susceptibility to Climate Change Impacts," factsheet (Gland, Switzerland: 2008).
42. J. Rockström et al., "A Safe Operating Space for Humanity," *Nature,* 24 September 2009, pp. 474–75.
43. Ibid.
44. Ibid.
45. Ibid.
46. Ibid.
47. Convention on Biological Diversity, "COP 6 Decision VI/26," The Netherlands, April 2002.
48. IUCN, op. cit. note 1.

GLACIAL MELT AND OCEAN WARMING DRIVE SEA LEVEL UPWARD (pages 43–46)

1. National Oceanic and Atmospheric Administration (NOAA), Global Sea Level Time Series, at ibis.grdl

.noaa.gov/SAT/SeaLevelRise/LSA_SLR_timeseries.php.

2. Ibid.; John Church, "Sea-Level Rise and Global Climate Change," *WCRP News* (World Climate Research Programme, 21 February 2008.

3. Anny Cazenave and William Llovel, "Contemporary Sea Level Rise," *Annual Review of Marine Science*, January 2010, pp. 145–73.

4. Ibid.

5. Intergovernmental Panel on Climate Change (IPCC), *Climate Change 2007: The Physical Science Basis. Contribution of Working Group I to the Fourth Assessment Report of the Intergovernmental Panel on Climate Change* (New York: Cambridge University Press, 2007).

6. Dennis P. Lettenmaier and P. C. D. Milly, "Land Waters and Sea Level," *Nature Geoscience*, July 2009.

7. A. Neftel et al., "Historical CO_2 Record from the Siple Station Ice Core," Carbon Dioxide Information Analysis Center (CDIAC), Oak Ridge National Laboratory (ORNL), at cdiac.ornl.gov/ftp/trends/co2/siple2.013; D. M. Etheridge et al., "Historical CO_2 Record Derived from a Spline Fit (20 Year Cutoff) of the Law Dome DE08 and DE08-2 Ice Cores," CDIAC, ORNL, at cdiac.ornl.gov/ftp/trends/co2/lawdome.smoothed.yr20; NOAA, "Use of NOAA ESRL Data," NOAA dataset, at ftp.cmdl.noaa.gov/ccg/co2/trends/co2_annmean_mlo.txt.

8. Neftel et al., op. cit. note 7; Etheridge et al., op. cit. note 7; NOAA, op. cit. note 7.

9. S. Levitus, J. Antonov, and T. Boyer, *Warming of the World Ocean, 1955–2003* (Silver Spring, MD: NOAA, 2005), Figure 3.

10. J. Hansen et al., "Global Land-Ocean Temperature Index," Goddard Institute for Space Studies, at data.giss.nasa.gov/gistemp/tabledata/GLB.Ts+dSST.txt.

11. Cazenave and Llovel, op. cit. note 3.

12. Ibid.

13. World Glacier Monitoring Service (WGMS), "Preliminary Glacier Mass Balance Data 2007/2008," at www.wgms.ch/mbb/sum08.html.

14. M. Zemp et al., *Global Glacier Changes: Facts and Figures* (Zurich: WGMS, 2008).

15. WGMS, op. cit. note 13, Figure 2.

16. Stacy Feldman, "Bolivia's Chacaltaya Glacier Melts to Nothing 6 Years Early," *SolveClimate*, 6 May 2009.

17. Ibid.

18. Aron Buffen et al., "Recently Exposed Vegetation Reveals Holocene Changes in the Extent of the Quelccaya Ice Cap, Peru," *Quaternary Research*, vol.

72 (2009), pp. 157–73.

19. Ibid.

20. "Observations: Changes in Snow, Ice and Frozen Ground," in IPCC, op. cit. note 5.

21. Calculated by authors, using standards given in IPCC, op. cit. note 5. This number agrees with the 56.6 meter figure given there and the 65 and 73 meter figures cited in Jane G. Ferrigno et al., "Coastal-Change and Glaciological Map of the Palmer Land Area, Antarctica: 1947–2009" (Reston, VA: U.S. Geological Survey, 2009).

22. U.N. Environment Programme (UNEP), *Climate Change Science Compendium, 2009* (Nairobi: 2009), p. 27; Ferrigno et al., op. cit. note 21.

23. Ferrigno et al, op. cit. note 21.

24. Ibid.

25. IPCC, op. cit note 5, p. 820. .

26. Ibid.

27. W. T. Pfeffer, J. T. Harper, and S. O'Neel, "Kinematic Constraints on Glacier Contributions to 21st-Century Sea-Level Rise," *Science*, 5 September 2008, pp. 1340–43; Stefan Rahmstorf, "A Semi-Empirical Approach to Projecting Future Sea-Level Rise," *Science*, 19 January 2007, pp. 368–70.

28. Glenn A. Milne et al., "Identifying the Causes of Sea-level Change," *Nature Geoscience*, June 2009, pp. 471–78.

29. Ibid.

30. David Anthoff et al., *Global and Regional Exposure to Large Rises in Sea-Level: A Sensitivity Analysis* (Norwich, U.K.: Tyndall Centre for Climate Change Research, October 2006).

31. Table 1 from the following: Pinaki Roy, "River Sediment May Counter Bangladesh Sea Level Rise," *Science and Development Network*, 4 May 2010; C. Loucks et al., "Sea Level Rise and Tigers: Predicted Impacts to Bangladesh's Sundarbans Mangroves," *Climatic Change*, January 2010, pp. 291–98; Gordon McGranahan, Deborah Balk, and Bridget Anderson, "The Rising Tide: Assessing the Risks of Climate Change and Human Settlements in Low Elevation Coastal Zones," *Environment and Urbanization*, April 2007, pp. 17–37; E. B. Capili, A. C. S. Ibay, and J. R. T. Villarin, "Climate Change Impacts and Adaptation on Philippine Coasts," Proceedings of the International Oceans 2005 Conference (Washington, DC: 2005), pp. 1–8; IPCC, *Climate Change 2007: Impacts, Adaptation and Vulnerability. Contribution of Working Group II to the Fourth Assessment Report of the Intergovernmental Panel on Climate*

Change (New York: Cambridge University Press, 2007); U.S. Environmental Protection Agency, "Coastal Zones and Sea Level Rise," at www.epa.gov/climatechange/effects/coastal/index.html, viewed 16 June 2010.

32. UN HABITAT, *State of the World's Cities 2008/2009: Harmonious Cities* (London: 2008), Chapter 3.3.

33. UNEP, *In Dead Water: Merging of Climate Change with Pollution, Over-Harvest, and Infestations in the World's Fishing Grounds* (Nairobi: February 2008), p. 32.

34. NOAA, Regional Sea-level Time Series, at ibis.grdl.noaa.gov/SAT/SeaLevelRise/LSA_SLR_timeseries_regional.php.

35. Ibid.

36. Table 2 from the following: John Roach, "Alps Glaciers Gone by 2050, Expert Says," *National Geographic News*, 23 January 2007; Augusto de la Torre, Pablo Fajnzybler, and John Nash, *Low Carbon, High Growth: Latin American Responses to Climate Change* (Washington, DC: World Bank, 2009); Azadeh Ansari, "Glaciers Disappearing from Kilimanjaro," *CNN*, at www.cnn.com/2009/TECH/science/11/02/kilimanjaro.glaciers/index.html, viewed 16 June 2010; Dan Morrison, "'Mountains of the Moon' Glaciers Melting in Africa," *National Geographic News*, 25 March 2008; "Himalayan Glaciers May Disappear by 2035," *Environmental News Network*, 11 November 2008; World Bank, "Kathmandu to Copenhagen: A Regional Climate Change Conference," 31 August 2009; Thomas Schueneman, "Alaskan Glaciers Really Are Shrinking," *Environmental News Network*, 8 August 2009.

37. International Centre for Integrated Mountain Development, *The Changing Himalayas: Impact of Climate Change on Water Resources and Livelihoods in the Greater Himalayas* (Kathmandu: 2009), p. 1.

38. Ibid.

39. Anna da Costa, "Conference Brings Attention to Himalayan Climate Threat," *Eye on Earth* (Worldwatch Institute), 14 September 2009.

40. Carolyn Kormann, "Retreat of Andean Glaciers Foretells Global Water Woes," *Yale Environment 360*, 9 April 2009.

41. Feldman, op. cit. note 16.

LOSSES FROM NATURAL DISASTERS DECLINE IN 2009 (pages 47–50)

1. Munich Re calculation, based on NatCatSERVICE database, 2010.

2. Munich Re, *Topics Geo: Natural Catastrophes 2008–Analyses, Assessments, Positions* (Munich: 2009), p. 35.

3. Ibid.

4. Munich Re, *Topics: Natural Catastrophes 2009–Analyses, Assessments, Positions* (Munich: 2010), p. XX.

5. Munich Re, op. cit. note 1.

6. Munich Re, op. cit. note 4.

7. Ibid.

8. Munich Re, op. cit. note 1.

9. Munich Re, op. cit. note 4.

10. Ibid.

11. Munich Re, op. cit. note 1.

12. Ibid.

13. Ibid.

14. Munich Re, op. cit. note 4; Munich Re, op. cit. note 1.

15. Munich Re, op. cit. note 1.

16. Munich Re, op. cit. note 4.

17. Ibid.

18. Ibid.

19. Ibid.

20. Ibid.

21. Ibid.

22. Munich Re, op. cit. note 1.

23. Munich Re, op. cit. note 4.

24. Munich Re, op. cit. note 1.

25. Ibid.

26. Ibid.

27. Ibid.

28. Ibid.

29. Ibid.

30. Ibid.

31. Ibid.

32. Ibid.

33. Ibid.

34. Ibid.

35. Ibid.

36. Ibid.

37. Ibid.

38. Ibid.

39. Ibid.

40. Ibid.

41. Ibid.

42. Ibid.

43. Ibid.

44. Ibid.

45. Ibid.

46. Ibid.

47. United Nations International Strategy for Disaster Reduction Secretariat (UNISDR), "Earthquakes Caused the Deadliest Disasters in the Past Decade," *News Brief* (Geneva: 28 January 2010).

BOTTLED WATER CONSUMPTION GROWTH SLOWS (pages 51–53)

1. John G. Rodwan, Jr., "Confronting Challenges: U.S. and International Bottled Water Developments and Statistics for 2008," *Bottled Water Reporter*, April-May 2009, pp. 15–16.
2. Ibid.; John G. Rodwan, Jr., "Bottled Water 2004: U.S. and International Statistics and Developments," *Bottled Water Reporter*, April-May 2005; Beverage Marketing Corporation of New York (BMC), "The Stats" (New York: 2002, 2005–07).
3. Rodwan, op. cit. note 1; Rodwan, op. cit. note 2; BMC, op. cit. note 2.
4. Rodwan, op. cit. note 1, p. 16.
5. Ibid.
6. Ibid., p. 13; Rodwan, op. cit. note 2; BMC, op. cit. note 2.
7. Rodwan, op. cit. note 1, p. 13.
8. Ibid.
9. Ibid., p. 16.
10. Ibid.
11. Ibid., pp. 15–16.
12. Ibid., p. 16.
13. Ibid., p. 16; BMC, 2006 and 2007, op. cit. note 2.
14. BMC, *2008 The Global Bottled Water Market* (New York: April 2009), Exhibit 1.8.
15. Rodwan, op. cit. note 1, p. 16.
16. Ibid.
17. Ibid.
18. Worldwatch calculation based on Rodwan, op. cit. note 1.
19. Ibid., pp. 16–17.
20. Ibid.
21. Ibid.; BMC, 2007, op. cit. note 2.
22. Rodwan, op. cit. note 1, p. 15.
23. "The Beverage World 100," *Beverage World*, October 2009, p. 20.
24. Rodwan, op. cit. note 1, p. 16.
25. Ibid., pp. 12–14.
26. Government Accountability Office (GAO), *Bottled Water: FDA Safety and Consumer Protections are Often Less Stringent than Comparable EPA Protections for Tap Water* (Washington, DC: June 2009), p. 2.
27. Rodwan, op. cit. note 1, p. 15.

28. Jennifer Cirillo, "Uncharted Waters," *Beverage World*, April 2009, p. S8.
29. Rodwan, op. cit. note 1, p. 16.
30. BMC, "Retail PET Holds Majority of U.S. Bottled Water," in *2009 The Value-Added Water Market in the U.S.* (New York: September 2009); BMC, *2009 Beverage Packaging in the U.S.* (New York: December 2009), Exhibit 1.14.
31. BMC, op. cit. note 14.
32. Plastics Europe, *The Compelling Facts About Plastics 2009* (Brussels: 2009), p. 13; American Chemical Council and Association of Postconsumer Plastic Recyclers, *2008 United States National Postconsumer Plastics Bottle Recycling Report* (Arlington, VA, and Washington, DC: 2009).
33. Andrew Kaplan, "Emerging Technologies: Bottling Nature," *Beverage World*, April 2009, pp. 76–77.
34. "PlantBottle Launches Globally," *Beverage World*, December 2009, p. 10; Chris Herring, "Coke's New Bottle is Part Plant," *Wall Street Journal*, 24 January 2010.
35. Herring, op. cit. note 34.
36. P. H. Gleick and H. S. Cooley, "Energy Implications of Bottled Water," *Environmental Research Letters*, 19 February 2009.
37. Ibid.
38. Ibid.
39. Ibid.
40. Ibid.
41. Olga Naidenko et al., *Bottled Water Quality Investigation: 10 Major Brands, 38 Pollutants* (Washington, DC: Environmental Working Group, 15 October 2008).
42. "Is Tap Water Safer than Bottled?" *Consumer Reports Safety Blog*, at blogs.consumerreports.org/safety/2009/07/is-tap-water-safer-than-bottled-water.html, 10 July 2009; GAO, op. cit. note 26, p. 7; "Since You Asked—Bisphenol A (BPA)," National Institute of Environmental Health Sciences, National Institutes of Health, at www.niehs.nih.gov/news/media/questions/sya-bpa.cfm, viewed 29 January 2010.
43. Cirillo, op. cit. note 28.
44. Marian Burros, "Fighting the Tide, a Few Restaurants Tilt to Tap Water," *New York Times*, 30 May 2007.
45. Sharon Pian Chan, "City of Seattle Won't Buy Bottled Water," *Seattle Times*, 13 March 2008; Cecilia M. Vega, "San Francisco: Mayor to Cut Off Flow of City Money for Bottled Water," *San Francisco Chronicle*, 22 June 2007.

46. "Bundanoon in 'World-First' Ban on Bottled Water," *The Australian*, 26 September 2009.

GRAIN PRODUCTION STRONG BUT FAILS TO SET RECORD (pages 56–58)

1. "Production-Crops," in U.N. Food and Agriculture Organization (FAO), *FAOSTAT Statistical Database*, at faostat.fao.org, updated 16 December 2009.
2. Ibid.
3. Ibid.
4. FAO, "Food and Agricultural Commodities Production: Top Production, World, 2008," at faostat.fao.org/site/339/default.aspx, viewed 30 August 2010.
5. FAO, op. cit. note 1.
6. FAO, *Food Outlook*, June 2010, p. 12.
7. Ibid., pp. 62–75.
8. Ibid.
9. Ibid.
10. Ibid.
11. Ibid.
12. Ibid.
13. Ibid.
14. Ibid.
15. Ibid.
16. Ibid.
17. FAO, op. cit. note 1; FAO, op. cit. note 6, p. 12.
18. FAO, op. cit. note 6, p. 12.
19. Ibid.
20. Ibid.; Organisation for Economic Co-Operation and Development and FAO, *OECD-FAO Agricultural Outlook 2010–2019 Highlights* (Paris: 2010), pp. 11–12.
21. FAO, op. cit. note 6, pp. 62–75.
22. U.S. Department of Agriculture (USDA), Economic Research Service (ERS), "Briefing Rooms – Corn," at www.ers.usda.gov/Briefing/Corn, updated 27 March 2009.
23. FAO, op. cit. note 6, pp. 62–75.
24. USDA, ERS, "Briefing Rooms – Corn: Trade," at www.ers.usda.gov/Briefing/Corn/trade.htm, updated 18 February 2009.
25. Ibid.
26. FAO, "Food Price Indices," Excel workbook available at www.fao.org/worldfoodsituation/FoodPrices Index/en, updated August 2010.
27. Ibid.
28. FAO, op. cit. note 6, p. 13.
29. Luzi Ann Javier, "Wheat Falls for Third Day in Chicago as Rally Deemed Excessive," *Bloomberg Businessweek*, 10 August 2010.

30. OECD and FAO, op. cit. note 20.
31. USDA, Foreign Agriculture Service, *Production, Supply, and Distribution*, online database, at www.fas.usda.gov/psdonline/psdQuery.aspx, custom query performed 24 August 2010.
32. FAO, op. cit. note 6, pp. 12–13.
33. Ibid., p. 12.
34. J. D. Glover et al., "Policy Forum Agriculture: Increased Food and Ecosystem Security via Perennial Grains," *Science*, 25 June 2010, pp. 1638–39.
35. OECD and FAO, op. cit. note 20, pp. 11–12.
36. FAO, "Post-harvest Losses Aggravate Hunger," press release (Rome: 2 November 2009).
37. Ibid.
38. Danielle Nierenberg, "Innovation of the Week: Investing in Better Food Storage in Africa," Worldwatch Institute Nourishing the Planet Blog, 21 January 2010.
39. OECD and FAO, op. cit. note 20, pp. 44–45.
40. Rodomiro Ortiz et al., "Climate Change: Can Wheat Beat the Heat?" *Agriculture, Ecosystems and Environment*, 7 March 2008, pp. 46–58.
41. Ibid.
42. Glover et al., op. cit. note 34.
43. Ibid.
44. Sophia Murphy, *Strategic Grain Reserves in an Era of Market Volatility* (Minneapolis, MN: Institute for Agriculture and Trade Policy, October 2009).
45. Ibid.; Rudy Ruitenberg, "Global Food Reserve Needed to Stabilize Prices, Researchers Say," *Bloomberg Businessweek*, 28 March 2010.
46. Murphy, op. cit. note 44; Ruitenberg, op. cit. note 45; Corazon T. Aragon, Flordeliza A. Lantican, and Ma. Eden S. Piadozo, "The United Nations Must Manage a Global Food Reserve," *UN Chronicle*, 1 April 2008.

MEAT PRODUCTION AND CONSUMPTION CONTINUE TO GROW (pages 59–62)

1. U.N. Food and Agriculture Organization (FAO), *FAOSTAT Statistical Database*, at apps.fao.org, updated September 2010; Organisation for Economic Development and Co-operation (OECD) and FAO, "Meat," *OECD AND FAO Agricultural Outlook 2010–2019* (Rome: June 2010), pp.147–58.
2. FAO, op. cit. note 1.
3. Ibid.
4. FAO, "Meat and Meat Products," *Food Outlook*, June 2010.

5. Ibid.
6. Ibid.
7. Ibid.
8. Ibid.
9. Ibid.
10. OECD and FAO, op. cit. note 1; FAO, op. cit. note 4.
11. FAO, op. cit. note 1.
12. OECD and FAO, op. cit. note 1.
13. Ibid.
14. FAO, op. cit. note 4.
15. FAO, *FAO Meat Monitor*, 1 September 2010.
16. OECD and FAO, op. cit. note 1.
17. FAO, op. cit. note 4.
18. OECD and FAO, op. cit. note 1.
19. Ibid.
20. FAO, op. cit. note 4; OECD and FAO, op. cit. note 1.
21. Food and Agricultural Policy Research Institute (FAPRI), *2010 U.S. and World Agricultural Outlook*, (Ames, IA: Iowa State University, 2010).
22. OECD and FAO, op. cit. note 1.
23. Ibid.; FAPRI, op. cit. note 21.
24. OECD and FAO, op. cit. note 1.
25. Ibid.
26. FAPRI, op. cit. note 21.
27. OECD and FAO, op. cit. note 1.
28. UNESCO, Scientific Committee on Problems of the Environment (SCOPE), and U.N. Environment Programme (UNEP), *Livestock in a Changing Landscape*. Policy Briefs No. 6, April 2008.
29. Ibid.
30. J. J. McDermott et al., "Sustaining Intensification of Smallholder Livestock Systems in the Tropics," *Livestock Science*, vol. 130 (2010), pp. 95–109; A Zezza et al., *Rural Household Access to Assets and Agrarian Institutions: A Cross Country Comparison*, Working Paper No. 07-17 (Rome: FAO Agricultural and Development Economics Division, 2007).
31. Mark Cackler et al., *Livestock Externalities: Public Policy and Investment Needs* (Washington, DC: World Bank, 2008); "NIGER: Forced to Sell Cattle for a Handful of Dollars," *IRIN News*, 22 June 2010.
32. OECD and FAO, op. cit. note 1.
33. UNESCO, SCOPE, and UNEP, op. cit. note 28.
34. Carolyn Imede Opio, "Impacts of Meat Consumption on Biodiversity," presentation at Green Week, Brussels June 2010; OECD and FAO, op. cit. note 1.
35. C. de Fraiture et al., "Looking Ahead to 2050: Scenarios of Alternative Investment Approaches," in *Water for Food, Water for Life: A Comprehensive Assessment of Water Management in Agriculture* (London and Colombo, Sri Lanka: Earthscan and International Water Management Institute, 2007), pp. 91–145.
36. Don Peden et al., "Water and Livestock for Human Development," in *Water for Food, Water for Life*, op. cit. note 35.
37. Jeannette van de Steeg et al., "Livestock and Climate Change," *Rural 21* (Nairobi: International Livestock Research Institute (ILRI), June 2009); Carlos Sere, "Livestock Food and Climate Change," *Issues* (ILRI), December 2009, pp. 40–44.
38. Joint FAO/International Atomic Energy Agency Programme, "Climate Change and the Expansion of Animal and Zoonotic Diseases—What is the Agency's Contribution?" at www-naweb.iaea.org/nafa/aph/stories/2010-climate-change.html.
39. World Health Organization (WHO), Global Alert and Response (GAR), "Cumulative Number of Confirmed Human Cases of Avian Influenza A/(H5N1) Reported to WHO," Geneva, 18 October 2010.
40. Ibid.
41. WHO, GAR, "Pandemic (H1N1) Weekly Update," Geneva, 23 July 2010; Donald G. McNeil Jr., "In New Theory, Swine Flu Started in Asia, Not Mexico," *New York Times*, 24 June 2009.
42. WHO, GAR, "Pandemic (H1N1) 2009—Update 112," Geneva, 6 August 2009.
43. Ibid.
44. World Organisation for Animal Health (OIE), "Foot and Mouth Disease, China (People's Rep. of) Follow-up Report 14," Paris, 2 August 2010, at www.oie.int/wahis/reports/en_fup_0000009560_20100802_164445.pdf.
45. OIE, "Foot and Mouth Disease, Botswana–Follow Up Report No. 4," 11 October 2010, at www.oie.int/wahis/public.php?page=single_report&pop=1&reportid=9576.
46. OIE, "Number of Reported Cases of BSE Excluding United Kingdom (since 1989)," at www.oie.int/eng/info/en_esbmonde.htm, last updated 11 October 2010; number of cases in the United Kingdom (including 1987 and prior), at www.oie.int/eng/info/en_esbru.htm, last updated 7 October 2010.
47. U.K. National CJD Surveillance Unit, "Monthly Statistics," 4 October 2010, at www.cjd.ed.ac.uk/figures.htm.
48. WHO, "Rift Valley Fever, Fact sheet N°207," revised May 2010, at www.who.int/mediacentre/factsheets/fs207/en/.

49. OIE, WAHID Interface, "Summary of Immediate Notifications and Follow-ups–2010: Rift Valley Fever," at www.oie.int/wahis/public.php?page=disease_immediate_summary&selected_year=2010.

50. WHO, GAR, "Rift Valley Fever," at www.who.int/csr/disease/riftvalleyfev/en/index.html.

51. Gardiner Harris, "Antibiotics in Animals Need Limits, F.D.A. Says," *New York Times*, 28 June 2010.

52. Holly Dolliver, Kuldip Kumar, and Satish Gupta, "Sulfamethazine Uptake by Plants from Manure-Amended Soil," *Journal of Environmental Quality*, vol. 36, no. 4 (2007), pp. 1224–30.

53. Tara Smith et al., "Methicillin-Resistant *Staphylococcus aureus* (MRSA) Strain ST398 Is Present in Midwestern U.S. Swine and Swine Workers," *Public Library of Science ONE*, 2009, vol. 4, issue 1 (2009).

54. Harris, op. cit. note 51.

55. Erik Eckholm, "U.S. Meat Farmers Brace for Limits on Antibiotics," *New York Times*, 15 September 2010.

56. Ibid.; U.S. Department of Health and Human Services, Food and Drug Administration, Center for Veterinary Medicine, "Draft Guidance The Judicious Use of Medically Important Antimicrobial Drugs in Food-Producing Animals," 28 June 2010.

57. Renata Micha, Sarah K. Wallace, and Dariush Mozaffarian, "Red and Processed Meat Consumption and Risk of Incident Coronary Heart Disease, Stroke, and Diabetes Mellitus, A Systematic Review and Meta-Analysis," *Circulation*, vol. 121 (2010), pp. 2271–83.

58. Anne-Claire Vergnaud et al., "Meat Consumption and Prospective Weight Change in Participants of the EPIC-PANACEA Study," *American Journal of Clinical Nutrition*, August 2010, pp. 398–407.

59. Danielle Nierenberg, "Biodiversity and Sustainable Meat Production and Consumption," presentation at Green Week, Brussels, June 2010.

60. Meatless Mondays Web site, at www.meatlessmonday.com; Allison Aubrey, "Campaign Aims to Make Meatless Mondays Hip," *National Public Radio*, 9 August 2010.

61. Jane Black, "Meatless Mondays, A Movement That Has Legs," *Washington Post,* 19 May 2010.

62. Ibid.

63. Secretariat of the Convention on Biological Diversity, "Genetic Diversity," in *Global Biodiversity Outlook 3* (Montréal: 2010).

64. Ibid.; Barbara Rischkowsky and Dafydd Pilling, eds., *The State of the World's Animal Genetic Resources for Food and Agriculture* (Rome: FAO, 2007).

65. Nierenberg, op. cit. note 59.

66. Ecoagriculture Partners, "Applying the Ecosystem Approach to Biodiversity Conservation in Agricultural Landscapes," *Ecoagriculture Policy Focus*, April 2008.

67. Henk Westhoek, "The Impact of Livestock on Biodiversity," presentation at Green Week, Brussels, June 2010.

GLOBAL FISH PRODUCTION CONTINUES TO RISE (pages 63–65)

1. U.N. Food and Agriculture Organization (FAO), *FAOSTAT Statistical Database*, at www.fao.org/fishery/statistics/software/fishstat/en, updated February 2010.

2. Ibid.

3. FAO, *The State of World Fisheries and Aquaculture 2008* (Rome: 2009).

4. Ibid.

5. Ibid.

6. Ibid.

7. Ibid.

8. Ibid.

9. Ibid.; FAO, *Food Outlook December 2009* at www.fao.org/docrep/012/ak341e/ak341e11.htm.

10. FAO, op. cit. note 3.

11. Ibid.

12. Ibid.

13. WorldFish Center (WFC), *WorldFish Annual Report 2008/2009* (Penang, Malaysia: 2009).

14. FAO, op. cit. note 3.

15. Ibid.

16. Ibid.

17. Ibid.

18. Ibid.

19. Michael Casey, "UN Wildlife Watchdog Considers Ban on Bluefin Tuna," *Associated Press*, 12 March 2010.

20. World Wildlife Fund (WWF), *Global Marine Program: High Seas* (Washington, DC: 2009).

21. Ibid.

22. Ibid.

23. FAO, op. cit. note 3.

24. Ibid.

25. "Chapter 12: Inland Fisheries and Aquaculture," in International Water Management Institute, *Water for Food, Water for Life: A Comprehensive Assessment of Water Management in Agriculture* (Colombo, Sri

Lanka: 2007).

26. FAO, op. cit. note 3.

27. Ibid.

28. Ibid.

29. Ibid.

30. Ibid.

31. Ibid.

32. Ibid.

33. WWF, *Salmon Aquaculture Dialogue* (Washington, DC: 2010).

34. WWF, *Shrimp Aquaculture Dialogue* (Washington, DC: 2010).

35. WWF, *Tilapia Aquaculture Dialogue* (Washington, DC: 2010).

36. Ibid.

37. Ibid.

38. Ibid.

39. WFC, op. cit. note 13.

40. FAO, op. cit. note 3.

41. Ibid.

42. Oceana, "Official Report Reveals that Salmon Aquaculture in Chile Uses 600 Times More Antibiotics than Norway," press release (Washington, DC: 24 July 2009).

43. Ibid.

44. FAO, op. cit. note 3.

45. Oceana, *Hungry Oceans: What Happens When the Prey is Gone* (Washington, DC: 2008).

46. FAO, op. cit. note 3.

47. Cam McGrath, "Egypt: A Big Catch Feeds Millions," *IPS–Inter Press Service*, 1 November 2009.

48. FAO, *Fisheries and Aquaculture in a Changing Climate* (Washington, DC: 2010).

49. Ibid.

50. Ibid.

51. Danielle Nierenberg, "Fishing for Recognition and Support," *Nourishing the Planet blog*, 10 December 2009, at blogs.worldwatch.org/nourishingtheplanet/fishing-for-recognition-and-support.

52. International Fund for Agricultural Development, *Inland Fisheries and Aquaculture* (Rome: 2009).

COCOA PRODUCTION CONTINUES GROWTH (pages 66–69)

1. "Production-Crops," in Food and Agriculture Organization (FAO), *FAOSTAT Statistical Database*, at faostat.fao.org, updated 16 December 2009.

2. Ibid.

3. Ibid. Several factors play into the area harvested each year, including political instability, disease, and tree damage.

4. Congressional Research Service, *Child Labor in West African Cocoa Production: Issues and U.S. Policy* (Washington, DC: 13 July 2005).

5. U.N. Conference for Trade and Development (UNCTAD), "Cocoa Uses," at www.unctad.org/infocomm/anglais/cocoa/uses.htm, viewed 12 August 2010.

6. "Production-Crops," op. cit. note 1.

7. Ibid.

8. Ibid.

9. Ibid.

10. Ibid.

11. Ibid.

12. Ibid.

13. Ibid.

14. Ibid.

15. "Cargill's Cocoa Road Show Details Crop Challenges," *Candy Industry*, 24 March 2010.

16. World Cocoa Foundation (WCF), "Southeast Asia," at www.worldcocoafoundation.org/what-we-do/southeast-asia.html, viewed 20 July 2010.

17. WCF, "Cocoa Market Update," compilation of latest reports and resources, October 2009, p. 2.

18. Ibid.

19. International Cocoa Organization (ICCO), "ICCO Monthly Averages of Daily Prices," online database at www.icco.org/statistics/monthly.aspx, viewed 16 July 2010.

20. Ibid.; Mike Stones, "Supply Worries Keep Cocoa Prices Rising," *ConfectionaryNews.com*, 14 June 2010.

21. UNCTAD, "New International Cocoa Agreement Concluded," press release (Geneva: 25 June 2010).

22. WCF, op. cit. note 17, p. 3.

23. Ibid.

24. Ibid.

25. AarhusKarlshamn (AAK), *Annual Report 2009* (Malmo: 2009), p. 23.

26. Directive 2000/36/EC of the European Parliament and of the Council of 23 June 2000 relating to cocoa and chocolate products intended for human consumption [Official Journal L 197 of 03.08.2001].

27. Food and Drug Administration (FDA), "FDA's Standards for High Quality Foods," *Consumer Update on Chocolate*, at www.fda.gov/ForConsumers/ConsumerUpdates/ucm094559.htm, 18 June 2007; Laura T. Coffey, "Chocoholics Sour on New Hershey's Formula," *MSNBC Today Show*, 19 September 2008; FDA, "Cacao Products," Code of Federal Regulations Title 21, Part 163.

28. Stones, op. cit. note 20; Caroline Scott-Thomas, "Chocolate Flavors Help Cushion Cocoa Price Impact," *ConfectionaryNews.com*, 24 November 2009.

29. AAK, op. cit. note 25.

30. Paul Rogers, "Special Report: Global Top 100," *Candy Industry*, 15 January 2009; Paul Rogers, "Global Confectionery Companies," *Candy Industry*, January 2009.

31. Mintel Global Market Navigator, "Chocoholics Unite as Chocolate Sales Worldwide Defy Recession," press release (Chicago: 23 December 2009).

32. Guy Montague-Jones, "Chocolate Sales Follow Suppliers to Eastern Europe, Says Report," *ConfectioneryNews.com*, 4 September 2009.

33. Ibid.

34. Euromonitor International, "Datagraphic: Chocolate Confectionery Retail Growth 2009–2010," *Euromonitor Global Market Research Blog*, 29 June 2010, at blog.euromonitor.com/2010/06/datagraphic-choc olate-confectionery-retail-growth-20092010.html #more.

35. ICCO, *Cocoa Resources in Consuming Countries* (London: May 2007), p. 25.

36. Ibid.

37. Ibid.

38. Ellen Pay, *The Market for Organic and Fair-Trade Cocoa* (Rome: FAO, September 2009), p. 5.

39. ICCO, *Quarterly Bulletin of Cocoa Statistics*, Vol. 36, No. 2, May 2010; ICCO, *Quarterly Bulletin of Cocoa Statistics*, Vol. 35, No. 2, May 2009; ICCO, *Quarterly Bulletin of Cocoa Statistics*, Vol. 33, No. 2, July 2007.

40. ICCO, May 2010, op. cit. note 39; ICCO, May 2009, op. cit. note 39; ICCO, July 2007, op. cit. note 39.

41. WCF, op. cit. note 17; Sustainable Tree Crops Program, "Cocoa," at www.treecrops.org/crops/cocoa.asp, viewed 16 July 2010.

42. WCF, op. cit. note 17.

43. Ibid.; WCF, "Learn About Cocoa," at www.worldco coafoundation.org/learn-about-cocoa, viewed 19 July 2010.

44. Augustine Ntiamoah and George Afrane, "Environmental Impacts of Cocoa Production and Processing in Ghana: Life Cycle Assessment Approach," *Journal of Cleaner Production*, 14 January 2008, pp. 1735–40.

45. Ibid.

46. Payson Center for International Development and Technology Transfer, *Second Annual Report: Oversight of Public and Private Initiatives to Eliminate the Worst Forms of Child Labor in the Cocoa Sector in Côte d'Ivoire and Ghana* (New Orleans: Tulane University, September 2008).

47. Ibid.

48. U.S. Department of State, *Trafficking in Persons Report June 2009* (Washington, DC: 2009); U.S. Department of State, *2009 Human Rights Report: Côte d'Ivoire* (Washington, DC: 11 March 2010); U.S. Department of State, *2002 Human Rights Report: Côte d'Ivoire* (Washington, DC: 31 March 2003).

49. Payson Center, op. cit. note 46, p. 10.

50. ICCO, "About ICCO," at www.icco.org/about/about.aspx, viewed 29 July 2010; ICCO, *Annual Report 2007/2008* (London: September 2008).

51. "Cargill's Cocoa Road Show," op. cit. note 15.

52. WCF, "What We Do," at www.worldcocoafounda tion.org, viewed 20 July 2010.

53. Catherine L. Alston, "Improving African Women's Access to Agriculture Training Programs," *Nourishing the Planet*, at blogs.worldwatch.org/nourishing theplanet/improving-african-women's-access-to-agriculture-training-programs, 17 May 2010.

54. "What Lies Ahead?" *Candy Industry*, 21 May 2010.

55. Fairtrade Foundation, "Consumers Purchase More Fairtrade Products than Ever Before," press release (Bonn: 26 May 2010).

56. "What Lies Ahead?" op. cit. note 54.

57. UNCTAD, op. cit. note 21.

58. Ibid.

59. Ibid.

60. Ibid.

FERTILIZER CONSUMPTION DECLINES SHARPLY (pages 70–72)

1. The International Fertilizer Industry Association (IFA), IFADATA, at www.fertilizer.org/ifa/ifadata/search, viewed 14 September 2010.

2. "World Fertilizer Prices Drop Dramatically after Soaring to All-Time Highs," *EurekAlert*, 16 December 2008.

3. Eric Sfiligoj, "Outlook 2010: Fertilizer," *CropLife.com*, January 2010.

4. "World Fertilizer Prices Drop," op. cit. note 2.

5. Patrick Heffer and Michael Prud'homme, *Fertilizer Outlook 2010–2014* (Paris: IFA, 2010), p. 2.

6. The Fertilizer Institute, "Fertilizer's Role in World Food Production," at tfi.org/factsandstats/fertilizer

andfood.cfm, viewed 15 September 2010.

7. U.N. Food and Agriculture Organization (FAO), *World Programme for the Census of Agriculture 2010* (Rome: 2007), p. 92.

8. Worldwatch calculation, based on data in IFA, op. cit. note 1, viewed 23 September 2010.

9. Ibid.

10. Ibid.

11. FAO, *Current World Fertilizer Trends and Outlook to 2013* (Rome: 2009), p. 9.

12. FAO, *Current World Fertilizer Trends and Outlook to 2011/12* (Rome: 2008), pp. 20–21.

13. Worldwatch calculation, based on data in IFA, op. cit. note 1, viewed 23 September 2010.

14. FAO, op. cit. note 12, p. 19.

15. U.S. Environmental Protection Agency, "Fertilizer Applied for Agriculture Purposes," in *2008 Report on the Environment*, at www.epa.gov/roe/index.htm.

16. Share is a Worldwatch calculation, based on data in IFA, op. cit. note 1, viewed 23 September 2010; Patrick Heffer and Michael Prud'homme, *Short-Term Fertilizer Outlook 2009–2010* (Paris: IFA, 2010), p. 3.

17. FAO, op. cit. note 12, p. 23.

18. Ibid.

19. Worldwatch calculation, based on data in IFA, op. cit. note 1, viewed 23 September 2010.

20. FAO, op. cit. note 12, p. 19.

21. Ibid., p. 25.

22. FAO, op. cit. note 12, p. 4; FAO, op. cit. note 11, p. 5.

23. FAO, op. cit. note 11, p. 5.

24. Population and changing diets from Canadian Fertilizer Products Forum, *Emerging Market Opportunities and Trends* (Ottawa: undated); 50 percent from FAO, op. cit. note 11, pp. 4–5.

25. FAO, *Livestock's Long Shadow, Environmental Issues and Options* (Rome: 2007), p. 44.

26. Canadian Fertilizer Products Forum, op. cit. note 24.

27. U.S. Department of Agriculture (USDA), National Agricultural Statistics Service, *Prospective Plantings* (Washington, DC: Agricultural Statistic Board, March 2009), pp. 1, 27.

28. USDA, Economic Research Service, "Supply and Use: Corn," in *Feed Grains Database*, at www.ers.usda.gov/Data/feedgrains, updated 1 December 2008.

29. Canadian Fertilizer Products Forum, op. cit. note 24.

30. FAO, op. cit. note 12, p. 7.

31. "Eutrophication," *The Encyclopedia of the Earth*, at www.eoearth.org/article/Eutrophication.

32. National Ocean and Atmospheric Administration (NOAA), "NOAA-Supported Scientists Predict 'Larger Than Average' Gulf Dead Zone," press release (Washington, DC: 28 June 2010).

33. Ibid.

34. Ibid.

35. James Elser and Stuart White, "Peak Phosporus," *Foreign Policy*, 20 April 2010.

36. Ibid.

37. Steven J. Van Kauwenbergh, *World Phosphate Rock Reserves and Resources* (Muscle Shoals, AL: International Fertilizer Development Center, 2010).

38. National Research Council, *Toward Sustainable Agricultural Systems in the 21st Century* (Washington, DC: 2010).

39. International Biochar Initiative, "What Is Biochar?" at www.biochar-international.org/biochar.

GLOBAL OUTPUT STAGNANT (pages 74–76)

1. Worldwatch calculation based on data in International Monetary Fund (IMF), *World Economic Outlook Database*, April 2010.

2. Ibid.

3. IMF, *World Economic Outlook* (Washington, DC: April 2010), p. 2.

4. Tim Callen, "PPP vs. the Market: Which Weight Matters," *Finance and Development*, March 2007.

5. Worldwatch calculation, op. cit. note 1.

6. Central Intelligence Agency, *The World Factbook* (Washington, DC: 2009).

7. IMF, op. cit. note 3.

8. Ibid.

9. Ibid.

10. Ibid.

11. Ibid., p. 47.

12. Ibid.

13. Ibid., pp. 6–7.

14. Environmental Protection Agency, *Municipal Solid Waste Generation, Recycling, and Disposal in the United States: Facts and Figures for 2008* (Washington, DC: 2009).

15. Sarah O. Ladislaw and Nitzan Goldberger, *Assessing the Global Green Stimulus*, briefing paper (Washington, DC: Center for Strategic and International Studies, February 2010).

16. World Bank, *World Development Report 2010* (Washington, DC: 2010), p. 59.

17. Ladislaw and Goldberger, op. cit. note 15.

18. Ibid.

19. Tsuyoshi Kawakami, *Cooperation with Asia and*

Pacific Islands: Toward A Sound Material Cycle Society (Tokyo: Office of Sound Material-Cycle Society Waste Management and Recycling Department, Ministry of the Environment, July 2008).

20. Ibid.

21. "Japan: Assessment and Recommendations," *OECD Environmental Performance Reviews*, May 2010.

22. World Bank, "Developing a Circular Economy in China: Highlights and Recommendations," policy note prepared by prepared by the Rural Development, Natural Resources and Environment Unit, East Asia and Pacific Region (Washington, DC: 2009).

23. Ibid.

24. Philipp Schepelmann, Yanne Goossens, and Arttu Makipaa, eds., *Toward Sustainable Development: Alternatives to GDP for Measuring Progress* (Wuppertal, Germany: Wuppertal Institute for Climate, Environment and Energy, 2010), pp. 52–56.

25. Austrian Ministry of Agriculture, Forestry and Water Management in cooperation with Sustainable Europe Research Institute, *What Kind of Growth is Sustainable?* (Vienna: 2009); United Kingdom from Sustainable Development Commission, *Redefining Prosperity* (London: 2009); France from Report by the Commission on the Measurement of Economic Performance and Social Progress, undated, at www.stiglitz-sen-fitoussi.fr/documents/rapport _anglais.pdf, 2009; European Union from *GDP and Beyond: Measuring Progress in a Changing World* (Brussels: 20 August 2009); Organisation for Economic Co-operation and Development, "Measuring the Progress of Societies," at www.oecd.org/pages/ 0,3417,en_40033426_40033828_1_1_1_1_1,00 .html.

26. Zhou Xin and Simon Rabinovitch, "Tired of Choking on Growth, China Launches Green GDP," *Reuters*, 4 November 2010.

27. Allegra Stratton, "Happiness Index to Gauge Britain's National Mood," (London) *Guardian*, 14 November 2010.

UNEMPLOYMENT AND PRECARIOUS EMPLOYMENT GROW MORE PROMINENT (pages 77–80)

1. International Labour Organization (ILO), *Global Employment Trends January 2010* (Geneva: 2010), p. 9.

2. Projection for 2010 unemployment from ILO, "Weak Employment Recovery with Persistent High Unemployment and Decent Work Deficits," published for the G20 Summit in Seoul, 11–12 November 2010, p. 3.

3. ILO, op. cit. note 1, p. 10.

4. Ibid., pp. 9, 12. Table 1 based on ibid., p. 46. The "advanced economies" encompass North America, the European Union (EU), a small number of West European countries that are not EU members (such as Switzerland and Norway), Japan, Australia, New Zealand, and Israel.

5. ILO, op. cit. note 1, p. 12.

6. Raymond Torres, "Incomplete Crisis Responses: Socio-economic Costs and Policy Implications," *International Labour Review*, vol. 149, no. 2 (2010), p. 231.

7. ILO, op. cit. note 1, p. 9.

8. Ibid.

9. International Institute for Labour Studies, *World of Work Report 2010: From One Crisis to the Next?* (Geneva: ILO, 2010), Executive Summary, p. 4.

10. Ibid., p. 1.

11. ILO, op. cit. note 1, p. 15.

12. Ibid.

13. Ibid., p. 16.

14. Ibid.

15. Ibid., p. 17.

16. Ibid., p. 14.

17. International Institute for Labour Studies, op. cit. note 9, p. vii.

18. ILO, op. cit. note 1, pp. 18–19.

19. Ibid.

20. Ibid., p. 54.

21. Ibid. To project 2009 figures, the ILO presents three scenarios. Here, we rely on data from the middle scenario.

22. Ibid.

23. Ibid.

24. Alan S. Blinder, "Outsourcing: Bigger Than You Thought," *American Prospect*, 22 October 2006.

25. Economic Policy Institute (EPI), *Datazone*, at www.epi .org/page/-/datazone2008/wage comp trends/pov erty_wages.xls.

26. EPI, *Datazone*, at www.epi.org/page/-/datazone2008/ wage comp trends/earnings.xls. Wages lagging behind productivity gains from EPI, *Datazone*, at www.cpi.org/page/ /datazone2008/wage comptrends/ prody_comp.xls.

27. Torres, op. cit. note 6, p. 228.

28. Ibid.

29. U.S. Bureau of Labor Statistics (BLS), "Economic News Release: Employment Situation Summary

Table A. Household Data, Seasonally Adjusted," press release (Washington, DC: 8 October 2010). BLS database offers a time series on unemployment trends at www.bls.gov/data/#unemployment.

30. BLS database, at www.bls.gov/data/#unemployment.

31. BLS, "Employment, Hours, and Earnings from the Current Employment Statistics survey (National)," at www.bls.gov/data/#employment, viewed 19 October 2010.

32. ILO, op. cit. note 2, p. 5.

33. Thorsten Kalina and Claudia Weinkopf, "Niedriglohnbeschäftigung 2008: Stagnation auf hohem Niveau–Lohnspektrum franst nach unten aus," *IAQ Bericht 2010-06* (Duisburg, Germany: Institut Arbeit und Qualifikation der Universität Duisburg-Essen), p. 7.

34. Ibid.

35. Ibid., p. 5.

36. Gerhard Bosch, "Lohnabstandsgebot: Arbeit muss sich lohnen," *Der Westen*, 14 February 2010.

37. Jan Goebel, Martin Gornig, and Hartmut Häußermann, "Polarisierung der Einkommen: Die Mittelschicht verliert," *Wochenbericht des DIW Berlin*, no. 24/2010, p. 6.

38. Wolfgang Lieb, "Privater Reichtum – öffentliche Armut," *NachDenkSeiten*, 23 June 2010.

39. Ibid.

40. Rate for 2010 from ILO, op. cit. note 2, p. 5; earlier rates from ILO, LABORSTA online database, at laborsta.ilo.org, data extracted 20 October 2010.

41. Machiko Osawa and Jeff Kingston, "Japan Has to Address the 'Precariat,'" *Financial Times*, 1 July 2010.

42. Ibid.

43. Julia Obinger, "Working on the Margins: Japan's *Precariat* and Working Poor," Discussion Paper 1, *Electronic Journal of Contemporary Japanese Studies*, 25 February 2009.

44. Osawa and Kingston, op. cit. note 43.

45. Torres, op. cit. note 6, p. 230.

46. Ibid.

47. Ibid.; Torres, e-mail to author, 3 November 2010.

MATERIALS USE UP (pages 81–83)

1. Worldwatch calculation based on data in Sustainable Europe Research Institute (SERI), at www.materialflows.net, viewed 10 November 2010.

2. Ibid.

3. Ibid.

4. Ibid.

5. 1900 from Mark Swilling and Marina Fischer-Kowalski, *Decoupling and Sustainable Resource Management: Scoping the Challenges* (Paris: Decoupling Working Group, International Panel for Sustainable Resource Management, U.N. Environment Programme (UNEP), March 2010 version), pp. 25–26; 2006 from SERI and Global 2000 (Friends of the Earth Austria), *Overconsumption?: Our Use of the World's Natural Resources* (Vienna: SERI, September 2009), p. 9.

6. SERI and Global 2000, op. cit. note 5, p. 7.

7. Swilling and Fischer-Kowalski, op. cit. note 5, pp. 25–26.

8. SERI and Global 2000, op. cit. note 5, p. 3.

9. Ibid.

10. Ibid.

11. Elke Pirgmeier, Friedrich Hinterberger, and Stefan Giljum, "What Kind of Growth Is Sustainable? Presentation of Arguments from a Policy Perspective," PowerPoint presentation at ECCB Prague, 3 September 2009, available at SERI.

12. Ibid.

13. Huib Wouters and Derk Bol, *Material Scarcity: An M2i study* (Delft, Netherlands: Materials Innovation Institute, November 2009).

14. Ibid.

15. Ibid.

16. "Rare Earths," in U.S. Geological Service, *Mineral Commodity Summaries* (Reston, VA: 2010).

17. Ibid.

18. Ibid.; Mark Grajam and Gopal Ratnam, "Rare Earth Prices Soar As China Quotas Hit Manufacturers Abroad," *Bloomberg Businessweek*, 15 November 2010.

19. Grajam and Ratnam, op. cit. note 18.

20. T. E. Graedel, lead author, *Metal Stocks in Society: Scientific Synthesis*, report for the International Panel for Sustainable Resource Management (Paris: UNEP, May 2010), pp. 18–19.

21. Ibid., p. 9.

22. Ibid.

23. Tsuyoshi Kawakami, *Cooperation with Asia and Pacific Islands: Toward A Sound Material Cycle Society* (Tokyo: Office of Sound Material-Cycle Society Waste Management and Recycling Department, Ministry of the Environment, July 2008).

24. "Japan: Assessment and Recommendations," *OECD Environmental Performance Reviews*, May 2010.

25. Ibid.

ROUNDWOOD PRODUCTION PLUMMETS
(pages 84–86)

1. Share is a Worldwatch calculation based on data from Food and Agriculture Organization (FAO), at faostat.fao.org.
2. Ibid.
3. Ibid.
4. Worldwatch calculation based on roundwood data from FAO, op. cit. note 1, and on population data from U.S. Bureau of the Census, *International Data Base*, electronic database, Suitland, Md.
5. Worldwatch calculation based on roundwood data from FAO, op. cit. note 1, and on population data from Census Bureau, op. cit. note 4.
6. Worldwatch calculation based on data in FAO, op. cit. note 1.
7. Ibid.
8. FAO, op. cit. note 1.
9. Ibid.
10. Ibid.
11. FAO, *State of the World's Forests 2009* (Rome: 2009), p. 70.
12. U.N. Economic Commission for Europe (UNECE), *Forest Products Annual Market Review 2008–2009* (New York: United Nations, 2009), Chapter 9.
13. FAO, *Global Forest Resources Assessment 2010: Key Findings* (Rome: 2010).
14. Ibid.
15. Ibid.
16. Ibid.
17. Ibid.
18. "Introduction," in Intergovernmental Panel on Climate Change, *Climate Change 2007: Mitigation* (Cambridge, U.K.: Cambridge University Press, 2007), p. 103.
19. FAO, op. cit. note 11, pp. 76-77.
20. Pervaze A. Sheikh, *Illegal Logging: Background and Issues*, Report for Congress (Washington, DC: Congressonal Research Service, 9 June 2008).
21. Ibid.
22. Ibid.
23. UNECE, Forest Products Annual Market Review 2008-2009, (New York and Geneva: United Nations, 2009); share is a Worldwatch calculation based on UNECE, this note, and FAO, Faostat, at faostat.fao.org/site/377/DesktopDefault.aspx?PageID=377
24. UNECE, op. cit. note 12.
25. Ibid.

26. FAO, op. cit. note 11, p. 74.
27. Ibid., p. 67.
28. Ibid.
29. Ibid.
30. Ibid., pp. 69–70.
31. Ibid., p. 62.
32. Ibid., p. 63.
33. Ibid., p. 74.

WORLD POPULATION GROWTH SLOWS MODESTLY, STILL ON TRACK FOR 7 BILLION IN LATE 2011
(pages 88–91)

1. U.N. Population Division, *World Population Prospects: The 2008 Revision, Population Database*, at esa.un.org/unpp, viewed 5 November 2010. Unless otherwise noted, all population data are from this database, in some cases with additional calculations based on them by the author.
2. Gross world product data from International Monetary Fund, *World Economic Outlook Database*, at www.imf.org/external/pubs/ft/weo/2010/02/weodata/index.aspx, viewed on 8 November 2010. If purchasing power parity is calculated, the developing world proportion of gross world product is much higher, at 48 percent.
3. Alexander Zhukov, deputy prime minister of Russia, "Russia and the World: Challenges for the New Decade," address to conference, 22 January 2010.
4. U.N. Development Programme, *Human Development Report 2010* (New York: 2010), p. 32.
5. Nicholas Eberstadt, "The Demographic Future," *Foreign Affairs*, November/December 2010, pp. 54–64.
6. Warren Sanderson and Sergei Scherbov Sanderson, "Remeasuring Aging," *Science*, 10 September 2010, pp. 1287–88.
7. Julia Whitty, "The Last Taboo," *Mother Jones*, May/June 2010, pp. 24–43.
8. Fertility data from U.N. Population Division, op. cit. note 1, and from ICF Macro/Measure DHS (Demographic and Health Surveys), available at www.statcompiler.com.

GLOBAL CHRONIC HUNGER RISES ABOVE 1 BILLION
(pages 92–95)

1. U.N. Food and Agriculture Organization (FAO), *The State of Food Insecurity in the World 2009* (Rome: 2009).
2. World Food Programme (WFP), "Hunger Stats," at

www.wfp.org/hunger/stats.

3. FAO, op. cit. note 1.

4. FAO, *FAO Statistical Yearbook 2006, Vol. 1* (Rome: 2006).

5. FAO, "Hunger–Basic Definitions," at www.fao.org/hunger/basic-definitions/en.

6. International Food Policy Research Institute (IFPRI), *2009 Global Hunger Index* (Washington, DC: 2009).

7. Ibid.

8. Ibid.

9. FAO, "Food Security Statistics by Country," at www.fao.org/cconomic/css/food-sccurity-statistics/food-security-statistics-by-country/en.

10. Ibid.

11. United Nations, *United Nations Millennium Declaration* (New York: 2000).

12. FAO, op. cit. note 1.

13. FAO, The State of Food Insecurity in the World 2008 (Rome: 2008).

14. Ibid.

15. Ibid.

16. Ibid.

17. IFPRI, op. cit. note 6.

18. Ibid.

19. Ibid.

20. World Bank, *World Development Report 2008: Agriculture for Development* (Washington, DC: 2008).

21. Ibid.

22. Ibid.

23. Ibid.

24. Ibid.

25. FAO, op. cit. note 1.

26. WFP, "Country Profiles: 2009," at www.wfp.org/countries.

27. Ibid.

28. U.S. Department of Agriculture (USDA), *Food Security Assessment 2008–2009* (Washington DC: 2009).

29. Ibid.

30. IFPRI, "2009 Global Hunger Index Calls Attention to Gender Inequality," press release (Washington DC: 14 October 2009).

31. FAO, op. cit. note 1.

32. IFPRI, op. cit. note 6.

33. World Health Organization, *Children: Reducing Mortality Fact Sheet* (Geneva: November 2009).

34. IFPRI, op. cit. note 6.

35. FAO, *How To Feed the World in 2050* (Rome: 2009).

36. The Food Price Index measures the price change of six commodity food groups (meat, dairy, cereals, oils, fats, and sugars) from one time period to the

next. Here, 2002/04 represents a time and food price base year.

37. USDA, op. cit. note 28.

38. IFPRI, op. cit. note 6.

39. Ibid.; U.S. Agency for International Development (USAID), "USAID's Office of Food for Peace 2009 Statistics," press release (Washington, DC: 10 January 2010).

40. FAO, *Climate Change and Food Security* (Rome: 2008).

41. Ibid.

42. World Bank, *Implementing Agriculture for Development: Action Plan FY2010–2012* (Washington, DC: 2009).

43. FAO, op. cit. note 35.

44. Pedro Sanchez et al., *United Nations Millennium Project Task Force on Hunger, Halving Hunger: It Can Be Done* (London: Earthscan, 2005).

45. FAO, op. cit. note 35.

46. WFP, "Countries: Haiti," at www.wfp.org/countries/haiti.

47. Ibid.

48. World Bank, *ARD News*, February 2010.

49. Prolinnova, "Ethiopia Country Programme," at www.prolinnova.net/Ethiopia.

50. World Vegetable Center, "vBSS: Vegetable Breeding and Seed Systems for Poverty Reduction in Africa," at avrdc.org/index.php?id=197.

51. USAID, "Sub-Saharan Africa: Zambia Overview," at www.usaid.gov/locations/sub-saharan_africa/countries/zambia/index.html.

52. International Fund for Agricultural Development (IFAD), "Eritrean Women Entrepreneurs Bring Additional Income to Their Families," at operations.ifad.org/web/guest/country/voice/tags/eritrea/eritreawomen.

53. IFAD, "Pioneering Microcredit for Women in Remote Pakistan," at www.ruralpovertyportal.org/web/guest/country/voice/tags/pakistan/microcredit.

EDUCATIONAL ATTAINMENT WORLDWIDE ON THE RISE (pages 96–98)

1. Educational attainment estimates for 1970–2000 by Wolfgang Lutz et al., "Reconstruction of Population by Age, Sex and Level of Educational Attainment of 120 Countries for 1970–2000," *Vienna Yearbook of Population Research*, vol. 2007 (Laxenberg, Austria: International Institute for Applied Systems Analysis (IIASA), 2007), pp. 193–235; educational attainment projections for 2005–2010 by Samir K.C. et

al., "Projection of Populations by Level of Educational Attainment, Age, and Sex for 120 Countries for 2005–2050," *Demographic Research*, vol. 22, no. 15 (2010), pp. 383–472; both datasets extrapolated by Worldwatch Institute to world population from United Nations Population Division, *World Population Prospects: The 2008 Revision Population Database*, at esa.un.org/unpp, viewed 13 July 2010.

2. Lutz et al., op. cit. note 1; K.C. et al., op. cit. note 1.

3. The educational attainment data used here are based on the IIASA-Vienna Institute of Demography (VID) dataset as applied to world population estimates compiled by the United Nations Population Division. The IIASA-VID data come from 120 countries, both industrial and developing, representing about 95 percent of the world's population from 1970 to 2010. Educational attainment proportions were assumed to be broadly representative of the remaining 5 percent of the world and applied to the U.N. Population Division population dataset to arrive at the total population figures used in this article. Five-year data series go back to 1970, grouping people into four categories based on the highest level of schooling they have achieved in their lifetimes: none at all, some primary, some secondary, and some higher (e.g., university) education. The data from 1970 to 2000 are estimates based on country-specific data on completed years of education among people aged 15 and older. Because of insufficient uniform raw data for this century, figures on educational attainment used here for 2005 and 2010 are from IIASA and VID projections based on the assumption of a continuation of twentieth-century trends. That assumption is borne out by the limited current educational-attainment data and school enrollment available.

4. Lutz et al., op. cit. note 1; K.C. et al., op. cit. note 1.

5. Lutz et al., op. cit. note 1; K.C. et al., op. cit. note 1.

6. Emily Hannum and Claudia Buchmann, *The Consequences of Global Educational Expansion: Social Science Perspectives* (Cambridge, MA: American Academy of Arts & Sciences, 2003); Wolfgang Lutz, "Sola Schola et Sanitate: Human Capital as the Root Cause and Priority for International Development?" *Philosophical Transactions of the Royal Society B*, no. 364, pp. 3031–47.

7. Hannum and Buchmann, op. cit. note 6; Lutz, op, cit. note 6.

8. Hannum and Buchmann, op. cit. note 6; Lutz, op, cit. note 6.

9. Lutz, op. cit. note 6.

10. Ibid.; Wolfgang Lutz, J. Crespo Cuaresma, and Warren Sanderson, "The Demography of Educational Attainment and Economic Growth," *Science*, 22 February 2008, pp. 1047–48.

11. Calculations by authors based on Lutz et al., op. cit. note 1.

12. Ibid.

13. Ibid.

14. Ibid.

15. Ibid.

16. Lutz et al., op. cit. note 1; K.C. et al., op. cit. note 1.

17. Lutz et al., op. cit. note 1; K.C. et al., op. cit. note 1.

18. Lutz et al., op. cit. note 1; K.C. et al., op. cit. note 1.

19. Lutz et al., op. cit. note 1; K.C. et al., op. cit. note 1.

20. Dina Abu-Ghaida and Stephen Klasen, "The Costs of Missing the Millennium Development Goal on Gender Equity," *World Development*, vol. 32, no. 7 (2004), pp. 1075–107.

21. Hannum and Buchmann, op. cit. note 6.

22. John Bongaarts, *Completing the Fertility Transition in the Developing World: The Role of Educational Differences and Fertility Preferences*, Working Papers No. 177 (New York: Population Council, 2003), pp. 1–27.

23. United Nations, "United Nations Issues Study on Women's Education and Fertility," press release (New York: 7 February 1996).

24. Robert Engelman, "Population & Sustainability," *Scientific American Earth* 3.0, summer 2009, pp. 22–29.

25. Ibid.

26. Dara Carr, *Is Education the Best Contraceptive?* Policy Brief (Washington, DC: Population Reference Bureau and Measure Communication, May 2000).

27. Ibid.

28. Teresa Castro Martin, "Women's Education and Fertility: Results from 26 Demographic and Health Surveys," *Studies in Family Planning*, vol. 26, no. 4 (July-August 1995), pp. 187–202.

29. Anne Moursund and Øystein Kravdal, "Individual and Community Effects of Women's Education and Autonomy on Contraceptive Use in India," *Population Studies*, November 2003, pp. 285–301.

30. Wardatul Akmam, "Women's Education and Fertility Rates in Developing Countries, with Special Reference to Bangladesh," *Eubios: Journal of Asian and International Bioethics*, vol. 12 (2002), pp. 138–43.

MOBILE PHONE AND INTERNET USE GROWS ROBUSTLY (pages 99–101)

1. Data for 1980–92 from International Telecommunication Union (ITU) as cited in World Bank, World Development Indicators database, at databank.worldbank.org, viewed 28 April 2010; 1993–2008 data from ITU, "Mobile Cellular Subscriptions," at www.itu.int/ITU-D/icteye/Indicators/Indicators.aspx#, viewed 28 April 2010; 2009 data from ITU, *Measuring the Information Society, 2010* (Geneva: 2010).
2. ITU, "Mobile Cellular Subscriptions," op. cit. note 1; ITU, *Measuring the Information Society, 2010*, op. cit. note 1; 2010 data from ITU, "Mobile Cellular Subscriptions to Reach 5 Billion Worldwide in 2010," *ITU News*, March 2010.
3. Data for 1993–97 from ITU as cited in World Bank, op. cit. note 1; 1998–2008 data from ITU, "Internet Indicators: Subscribers, Users, and Broadband Subscribers," at www.itu.int/ITU-D/icteye/Indicators/Indicators.aspx#, viewed 28 April 2010; 2009 data from ITU, *Measuring the Information Society, 2010*, op. cit. note 1.
4. ITU, "Mobile Cellular Subscriptions," op. cit. note 1; ITU, *Measuring the Information Society, 2010*, op. cit. note 1.
5. ITU, *Measuring the Information Society, 2010*, op. cit. note 1; ITU, "Mobile Telephone Subscribers Per 100 Inhabitants, 1997–2007," at www.itu.int/ITU-D/ict/statistics/ict/graphs/mobile.jpg, viewed 25 May 2010.
6. ITU, "Mobile Cellular Subscriptions," op. cit. note 1.
7. Ibid.
8. Ibid.
9. Ibid.
10. Ibid.
11. Ibid.
12. ITU, *Measuring the Information Society, 2010*, op. cit. note 1.
13. ITU, op. cit. note 3.
14. Ibid.
15. Ibid.
16. ITU, "Mobile Cellular Subscriptions to Reach 5 Billion," op. cit. note 2.
17. Ineum Consulting as cited in Cyril Altmeyer, "Smartphones, Social Networks to Boost Mobile Advertising," *Reuters,* 29 June 2009.
18. "Metals Without Mining," in Gunter Pauli, *The Blue Economy* (Taos, NM: Paradigm Publications, 2010).
19. U.S. Environmental Protection Agency, "Statistics on the Management of Used and End-of-Life Electronics," at www.epa.gov/wastes/conserve/materials/ecycling/manage.htm, viewed 30 May 2010; Larry Greenemeier, "Trashed Tech: Where Do Old Cell Phones, TVs and PCs Go to Die?" *Scientific American*, 29 November 2007.
20. United Nations University, "Set World Standards for Electronics Recycling, Reuse to Curb E-waste Exports to Developing Countries, Experts Urge," *ScienceDaily*, 17 September 2009.
21. Basel Action Network, "Major Corporations Step Up For Green Certified Electronics Recycling," press release (Seattle, WA: 15 April 2010).
22. Basel Action Network, "e-Stewards Certification Introduction," April 2010, at e-stewards.org/certification-overview, viewed 15 May 2010.
23. Basel Action Network, op. cit. note 21.
24. Facebook, "Press Room," at www.facebook.com/press/info.php?statistics, viewed 27 June 2010.
25. Alison Fennah, "The Definitive European Media Consumption Study—Presentation for Web," *Mediascope Europe,* at www.slideshare.net/victori98pt/the-definitive-european-media-consumption-study; viewed 16 May 2010; Harris Interactive, "Internet Users Now Spending an Average of 13 Hours a Week Online," press release (New York: 23 December 2009).
26. Kevin J. O'Brien, "Sunset for the European Mobile Phone Industry?" *New York Times*, 10 February 2008.
27. Mobile Data Association, "The Q4 2009 UK Mobile Trends Report: UK Sends 11 Million Text Messages an Hour," press release (Sleaford, U.K.: 28 January 2010).
28. Kaiser Family Foundation, "Daily Media Use Among Children and Teens Up Dramatically from Five Years Ago," press release (Washington, DC: 20 January 2010); Victoria J. Rideout, Ulla G. Foehr, and Donald F. Roberts, *Generation M2: Media in the Lives of 8- to 18-Year-Olds* (Washington, DC: Kaiser Family Foundation, January 2010).
29. Adam Gabbatt, "Excessive Internet Use Linked to Depression, Research Shows," (London) *Guardian*, 3 February 2010.
30. Douglas Rushkoff, "South Korea: The Most Wired Place on Earth," *Frontline: Digital_Nation*, 14 April 2009; Geoffrey Cain, "South Korea Cracks Down on Gaming Addiction," *Time*, 20 April 2010.
31. National Safety Council, *Understanding the Distracted Brain: Why Driving While Using Hands-free*

Cell Phones Is Risky Behavior (Itasca, IL: March 2010); Matt Richtel, "In Study, Texting Lifts Crash Risk by Large Margin," *New York Times,* 27 July 2009.

32. National Safety Council, op. cit. note 31.
33. Ibid.
34. Ibid.
35. Dan Whitcomb, "U.S. Teens Ignore Laws Against Texting While Driving," *Reuters,* 11 December 2009.
36. Vaughn Hester, "CrowdFlower Impacts the Future of Disaster Relief," *Haiti Rewired,* 23 April 2010; Caroline Preston, Nicole Wallace, and Ian Wilhelm, "American Charities Raise Close to $1-Billion for Haiti, Chronicle Tally Finds," *The Chronicle of Philanthropy,* 16 March 2010.
37. "Text Message Surgery Saves Teenager's Life," *CNN News,* 13 January 2009.
38. Safaricom, *M-PESA Key Performance Statistics* (17 February 2010), at ; John Mulrow, "Think Mobile, Act Local," *World Watch,* May/June 2010, p. 24.
39. Safaricom, op. cit. note 38; currency converter KES to dollars, 28 May 2010, at www.xe.com.
40. Sarfaricom, *M_Kesho FAQ's,* at www.safaricom.co.ke/fileadmin/template/main/downloads/m-pesa_resource_centre/mkesho_FAQs/M-KESHO%20FAQS.pdf, viewed 25 June 2010.
41. Mulrow, op. cit. note 38, p. 25.
42. Gene Koprowski, "Wireless World: The 'Orange Revolution,'" *UPI,* 27 December 2004.
43. Kristin Schall, "The Revolution Will Be Tweeted: Activism in the Age of User Generated Content," *CommonDreams.org,* 29 June 2009; Radio Free Europe/Radio Liberty, "Moldova's 'Twitter Revolution,'" 8 April 2009; Luke Harding, "Moldova Forces Regain Control of Parliament after 'Twitter revolution,'" (London) *Guardian,* 8 April 2009.

The Vital Signs Series

Some topics are included each year in *Vital Signs*; others are covered only in certain years. The following is a list of topics covered in *Vital Signs* thus far, with the year or years they appeared indicated in parentheses. The reference to 2006 indicates *Vital Signs 2006–2007*; 2007 refers to *Vital Signs 2007–2008*.

ENERGY AND TRANSPORTATION

Fossil Fuels
    Carbon Use (1993)
    Coal (1993–96, 1998, 2009, 2011)
    Fossil Fuels Combined (1997, 1999–2003, 2005–07, 2010)
    Natural Gas (1992, 1994 96, 1998, 2011)
    Oil (1992–96, 1998, 2009)
Renewables, Efficiency, Other Sources
    Biofuels (2005–07, 2009–11)
    Biomass Energy (1999)
    Combined Heat and Power (2009)
    Compact Fluorescent Lamps (1993–96, 1998–2000, 2002, 2009)
    Efficiency (1992, 2002, 2006)
    Geothermal Power (1993, 1997)
    Hydroelectric Power (1993, 1998, 2006)
    Nuclear Power (1992–2003, 2005–07, 2009, 2011)
    Solar Power (1992–2002, 2005–07, 2009–11)
    Solar Thermal Power (2010)
    Wind Power (1992–2003, 2005–07, 2009–11)
Transportation
    Air Travel (1993, 1999, 2005–07, 2011)
    Bicycles (1992–2003, 2005–07, 2009)
    Car-sharing (2002, 2006)
    Electric Cars (1997)
    Gas Prices (2001)
    Motorbikes (1998)
    Railroads (2002)
    Urban Transportation (1999, 2001)
    Vehicles (1992–2003, 2005–07, 2009–11)

ENVIRONMENT AND CLIMATE

Atmosphere and Climate
    Carbon Emissions (1992, 1994–2002, 2009)
    Carbon and Temperature Combined (2003, 2005–07, 2009–10)
    CFC Production (1992–96, 1998, 2002)
    Global Temperature (1992–2002)
    Ozone Layer (1997, 2007)
    Sea Level Rise (2003, 2011)
    Weather-related Disasters (1996–2001, 2003, 2005–07, 2009–11)
Natural Resources, Animals, Plants
    Amphibians (1995, 2000)
    Aquatic Species (1996, 2002)
    Birds (1992, 1994, 2001, 2003, 2006)
    Coral Reefs (1994, 2001, 2006, 2010)

FOOD AND AGRICULTURE

GLOBAL ECONOMY AND RESOURCES

Gold (1994, 2000, 2007)
Illegal Drugs (2003)
Materials Use (2011)
Metals Exploration (1998, 2002)
Metals Production (2002, 2010)
Paper (1993–94, 1998–2000)
Paper Recycling (1994, 1998, 2000)
Roundwood (1994, 1997, 1999, 2002, 2006–07, 2011)
Steel (1993, 1996, 2005–07)
Steel Recycling (1992, 1995)
Subsidies for Environmental Harm (1997)
Wheat/Oil Exchange Rate (1992–93, 2001)
World Economy and Finance
Agribusiness (2007)
Agricultural Trade (2001)
Aid for Sustainable Development (1997, 2002)
Carbon Markets (2009)
Developing-Country Debt (1992–95, 1999–2003)
Environmental Taxes (1996, 1998, 2000)
Food Aid (1997)
Global Economy (1992–2003, 2005–07, 2009–11)
Green Jobs (2000, 2009)
Microcredit (2001, 2009)
Private Finance in Third World (1996, 1998, 2005)
R&D Expenditures (1997)
Seafood Prices (1993)
Socially Responsible Investing (2001, 2005, 2007)
Stock Markets (2001)
Trade (1993–96, 1998–2000, 2002, 2005)
Transnational Corporations (1999–2000)
U.N. Finances (1998–99, 2001)
Other Economic Topics
Advertising (1993, 1999, 2003, 2006, 2010)
Charitable Donations (2002)
Child Labor (2007)
Cigarette Taxes (1993, 1995, 1998)
Corporate Responsibility (2006)

Cruise Industry (2002)
Ecolabeling (2002)
Government Corruption (1999, 2003)
Informal Economies (2007)
Labor Force (2010)
Nanotechnology (2006)
Pay Levels (2003)
Pharmaceutical Industry (2001)
PVC Plastic (2001)
Satellite Monitoring (2000)
Television (1995)
Tourism (2000, 2003, 2005)
Unemployment (1999, 2005, 2011)

POPULATION AND SOCIETY

Communications
Computer Production and Use (1995)
Internet (1998–2000, 2002)
Internet and Telephones Combined (2003, 2006–07, 2011)
Satellites (1998–99)
Telephones (1998–2000, 2002)
Health
AIDS/HIV Incidence (1994–2003, 2005–07)
Alternative Medicine (2003)
Asthma (2002)
Avian Flu (2007)
Breast and Prostate Cancer (1995)
Child Mortality (1993, 2009)
Cigarettes (1992–2001, 2003, 2005)
Drug Resistance (2001)
Endocrine Disrupters (2000)
Fast-Food Use (1999)
Food Safety (2002)
Health Aid Funding (2010)
Health Care Spending (2001)
Hunger (1995, 2011)
Immunizations (1994)
Infant Mortality (1992, 2006)
Infectious Diseases (1996)
Life Expectancy (1994, 1999)
Malaria (2001, 2007)

Malnutrition (1999)
Mental Health (2002)
Mortality Causes (2003)
Noncommunicable Diseases (1997)
Obesity (2001, 2006)
Polio (1999)
Sanitation (1995, 1998, 2006, 2010)
Soda Consumption (2002)
Traffic Accidents (1994)
Tuberculosis (2000)
Military
Armed Forces (1997)
Arms Production (1997)
Arms Trade (1994)
Landmines (1996, 2002)
Military Expenditures (1992, 1998, 2003, 2005–06)
Nuclear Arsenal (1992–96, 1999, 2001, 2005, 2007)
Peacekeeping Expenditures (1994–2003, 2005–07, 2009)
Resource Wars (2003)
Wars (1995, 1998–2003, 2005–07)
Small Arms (1998–99)
Reproductive Health and Women's Status
Family Planning Access (1992)
Female Education (1998)
Fertility Rates (1993)
Maternal Mortality (1992, 1997, 2003)
Population Growth (1992–2003, 2005–07, 2009–11)

Sperm Count (1999, 2007)
Violence Against Women (1996, 2002)
Women in Politics (1995, 2000)
Other Social Topics
Aging Populations (1997)
Educational Levels (2011)
Homelessness (1995)
Income Distribution or Poverty (1992, 1995, 1997, 2002–03, 2010)
Language Extinction (1997, 2001, 2006)
Literacy (1993, 2001, 2007)
International Criminal Court (2003)
Millennium Development Goals (2005, 2007)
Nongovernmental Organizations (1999)
Orphans Due to AIDS Deaths (2003)
Prison Populations (2000)
Public Policy Networks (2005)
Quality of Life (2006)
Refugees (1993–2000, 2001, 2003, 2005)
Refugees-Environmental (2009)
Religious Environmentalism (2001)
Slums (2006)
Social Security (2001)
Sustainable Communities (2007)
Teacher Supply (2002)
Urbanization (1995–96, 1998, 2000, 2002, 2007)
Voter Turnouts (1996, 2002)